A bo
about
whales

Andrea Antinori

Corraini
Edizioni

The man here doesn't know it.
But there is a **humpback whale** there just underneath his boat, where he is sitting quietly.
It seems very interested in his hook.
There would be a problem if it swallowed the bait.
Do you think the whale would eat the man?
Of course not! That's not the case at all, **humpback whales** are good. They don't eat people!
The problem is that the man would fall into the water. **Humpback whales** are too heavy to pull up.
Wait a minute, I almost forgot...

Do you know what a humpback whale is?
You do? How do you already know?
Oh, of course, that's right. If you opened this book, you must really love whales!
But, I'm sure, there are still a lot of things you don't know.
Calm down, I didn't mean to get you down.
It's just that I'm very chatty and as you read through these pages, I'll tell you everything I have learnt about **humpback whales**, and all the other kinds of whales.

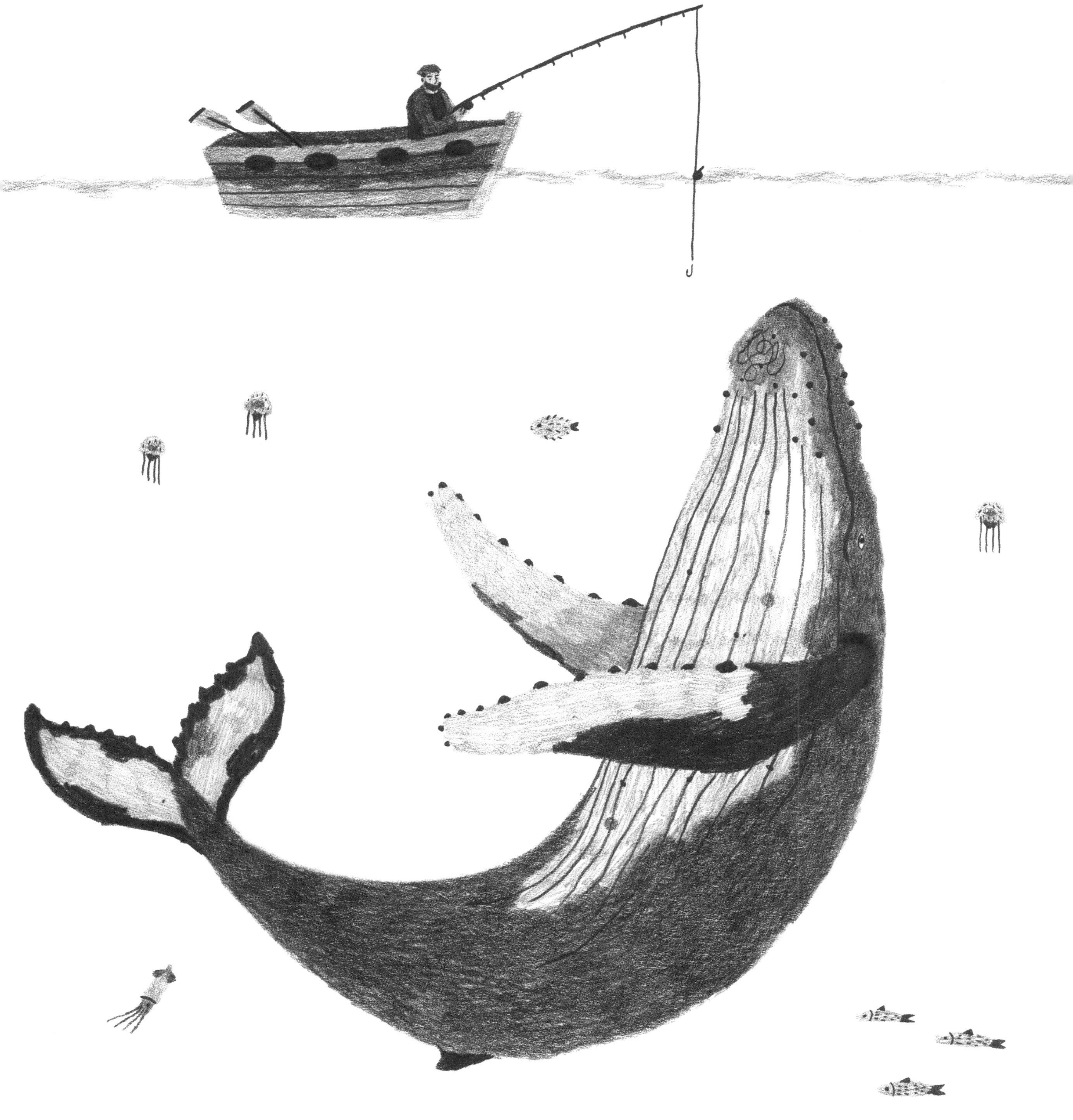

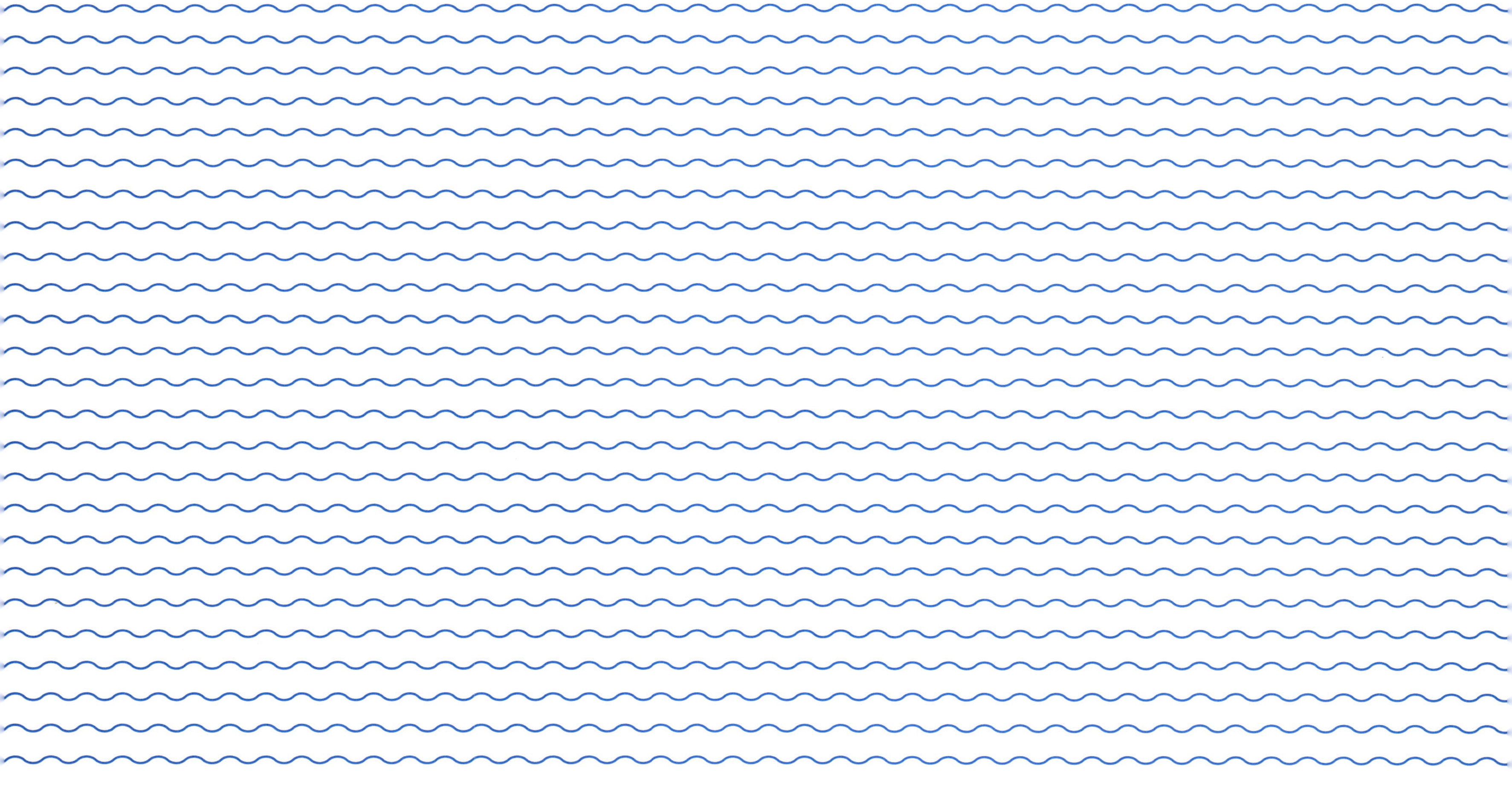

In general

Aren’t they fish?

No, sir.
Whales are **mammals**, just like us. In particular, along with dolphins, they belong to the **cetacean** order; mammals who spend their entire lives underwater.

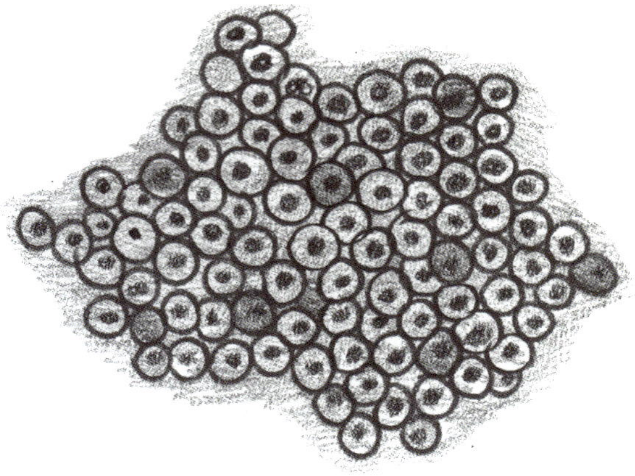

So what does it mean that they are mammals?
Unlike fish, whales have **mammary glands** and they suckle their young after **birth**.
Fish, on the other hand, lay their **eggs** and when the baby fish are ready to leave, they are already able to feed themselves.

Mammals are **warm-blooded** animals, that means they are able to control their own body temperature.
Fish, on the other hand, are **cold-blooded** and that means their body temperature varies in relation to the environment in which they swim.

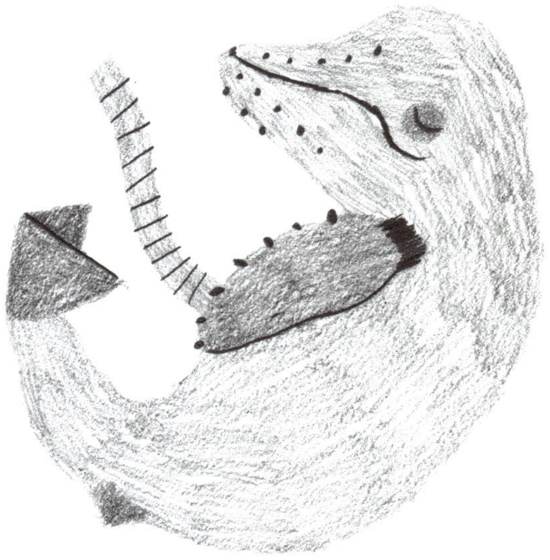

Not all of them, though!
Some fish, such as tuna, swordfish and some species of shark, have an independent body temperature system, just like mammals.

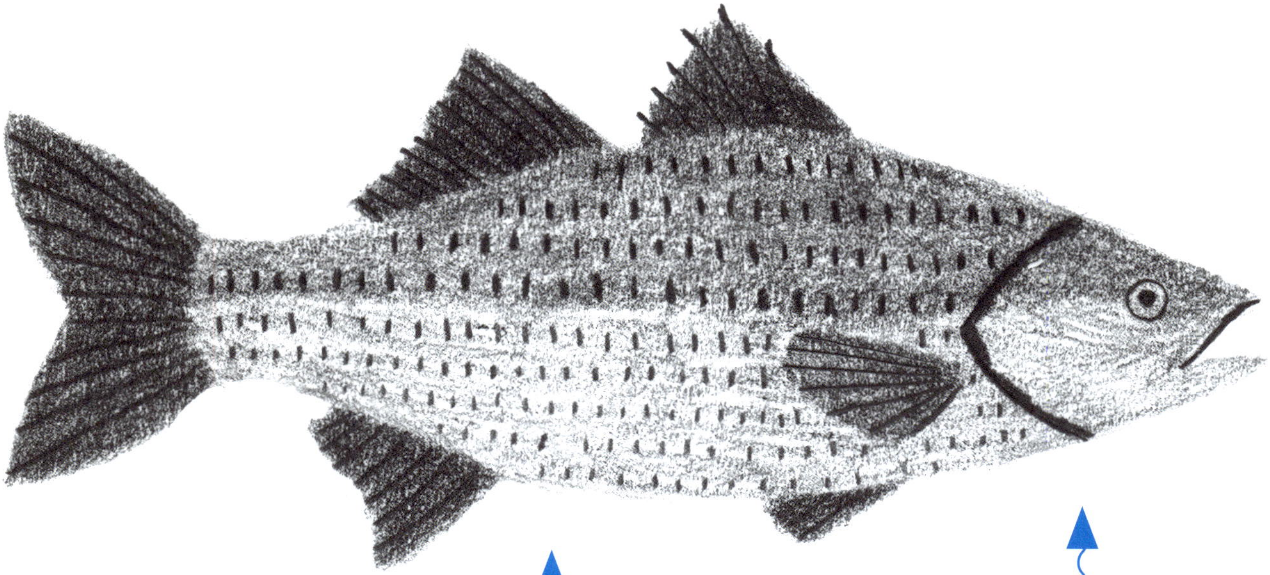

Cetaceans have **horizontal tails** that move up and down, whereas fish have **vertical tails** that move from left to right.

Whale **skin** is **smooth** like human skin, but fish skin is covered with **hard scales**.

Whales have **lungs** and a **blowhole** and it works in the same way as our noses. That's why they need to go to the surface to breathe. Fish extract oxygen from water through their **gills**.

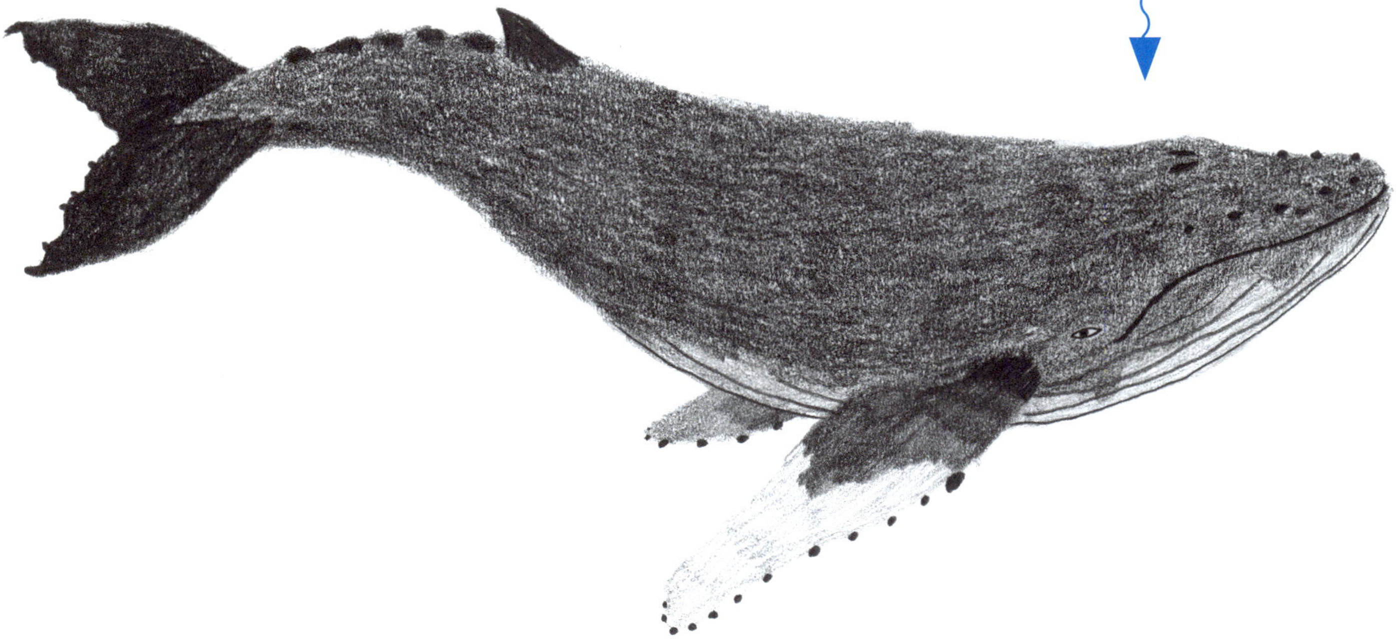

A good imitator

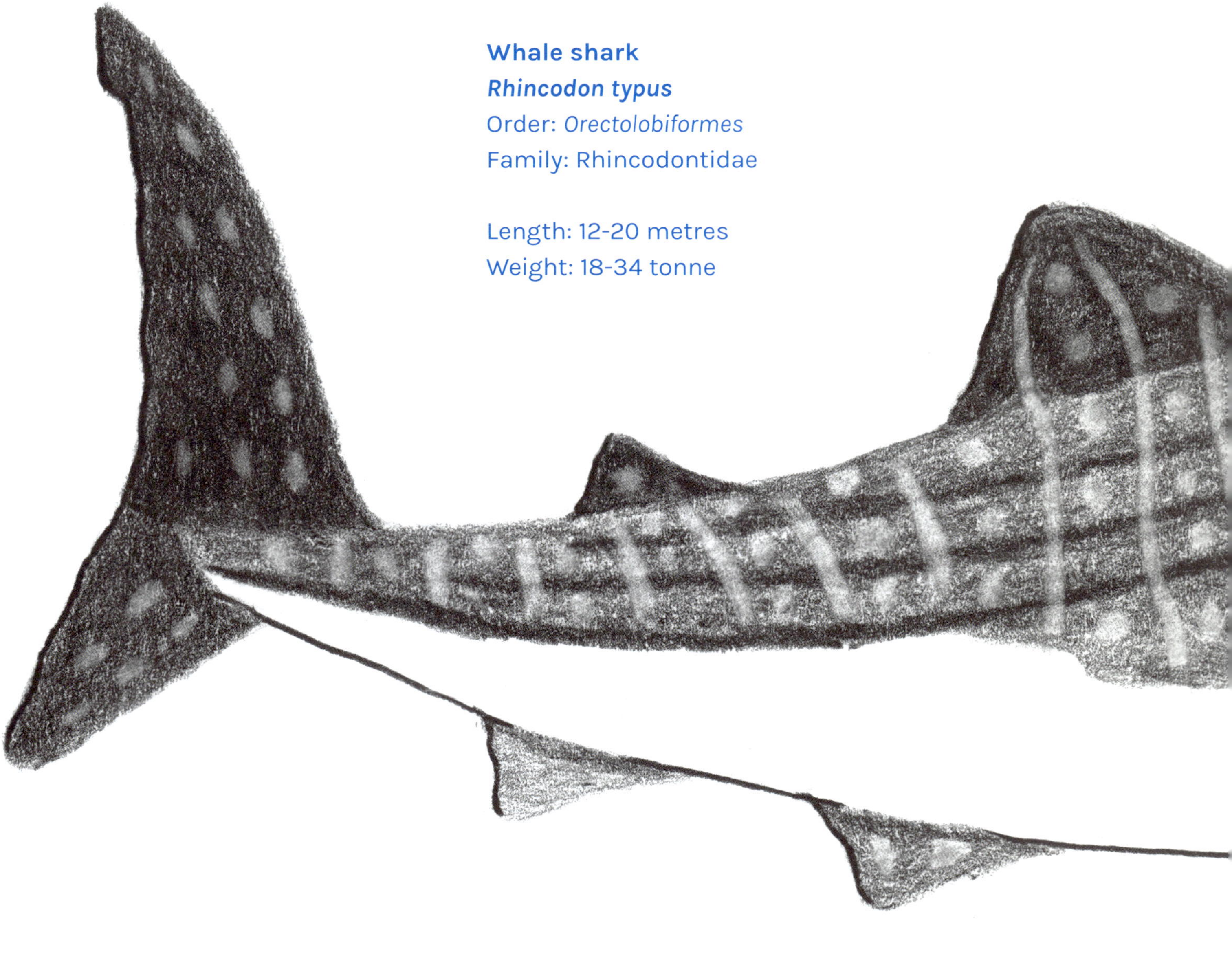

Whale shark
Rhincodon typus
Order: *Orectolobiformes*
Family: Rhincodontidae

Length: 12-20 metres
Weight: 18-34 tonne

There is a shark who wants to look like a whale so much, it has become as large as one! I'm talking about the **whale shark**, the largest fish in the world. Don't get too frightened though, it is completely peaceful towards humans. To be like a whale, you have to eat like a whale: unlike other sharks, whale sharks do not feed on other large animals but, like whales, they prefer to eat tiny crustaceans that are carried into their mouths by the currents. Don't forget that the whale shark is still a **fish** in all respects, it uses **gills** to breathe and the young hatch from **eggs** even if they hatch inside the body.

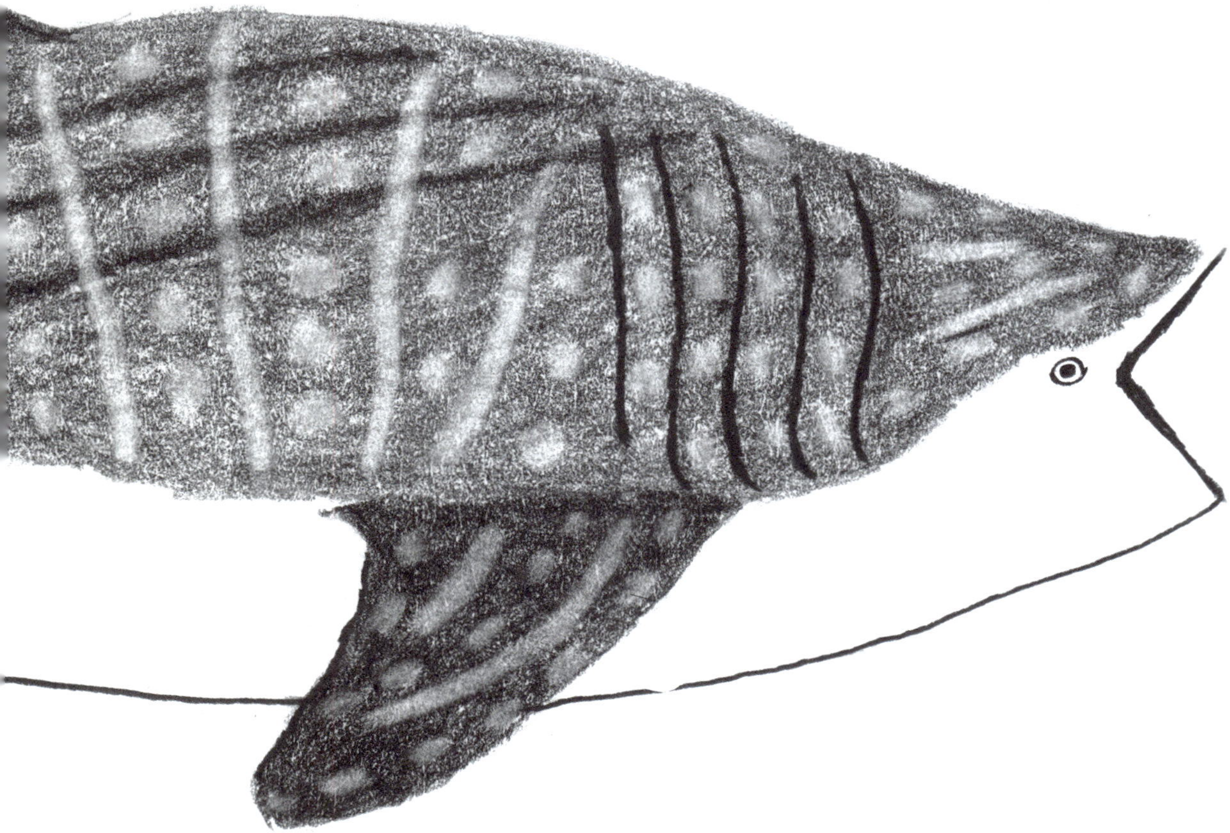

Baleen...

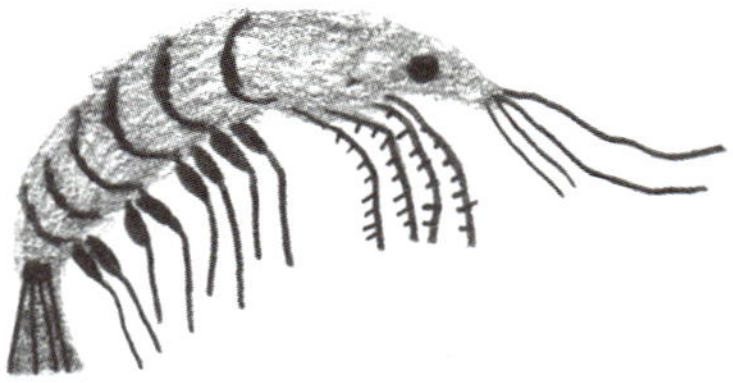

Cetaceans are divided into two main groups: **baleen** and **toothed**.

What are baleen whales?
And what are toothed whales?

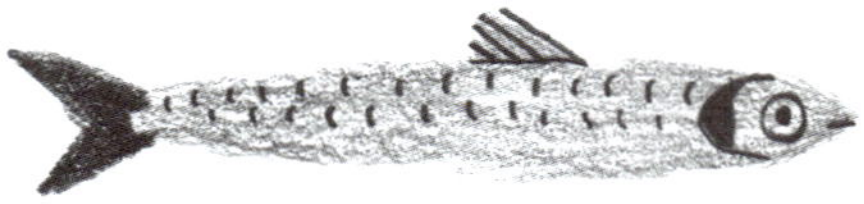

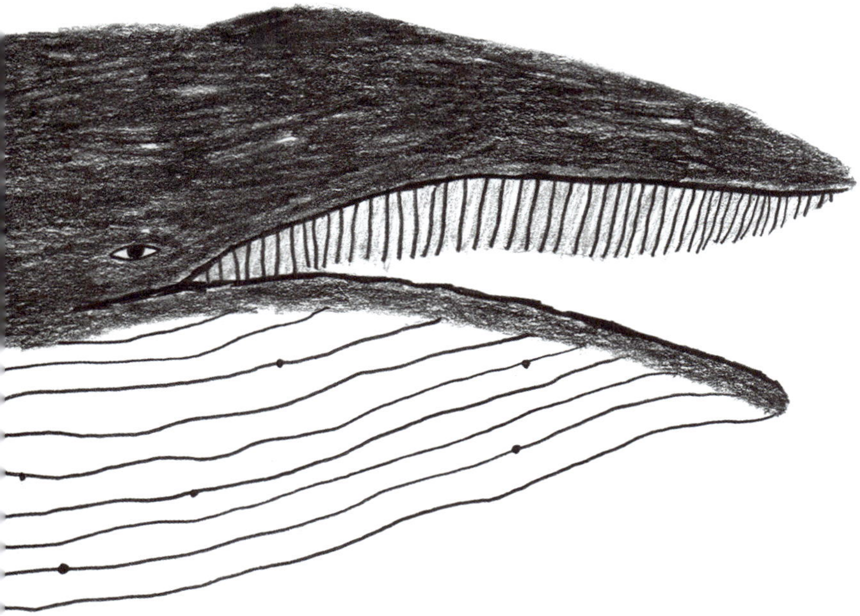

Baleen whales

Baleen whales are more similar to our idea of a whale, mainly because, in the majority of cases, they are also the larger ones. They have that name because, instead of teeth, they have a **baleen plate** (the taxonomic name, *mysticeti*, means "whale with moustache" in Greek), long plates that hang from the top of the mouth. Baleen whales only eat tiny animals like **krill** (a type of prawn) or small fish, they don't need teeth to grab or bite them. **Baleen plates** are very useful as they are used to help separate food from seawater. There are just 11 different species of baleen whale, compared to 70 different types of toothed whale.

Have you noticed?
Baleen plates look like the teeth on a comb!

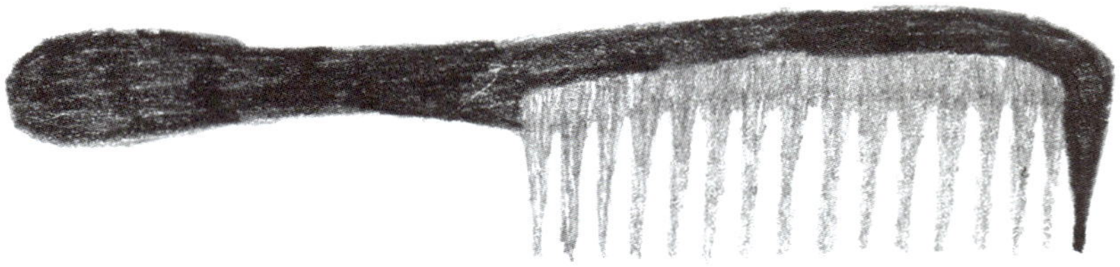

or toothed?

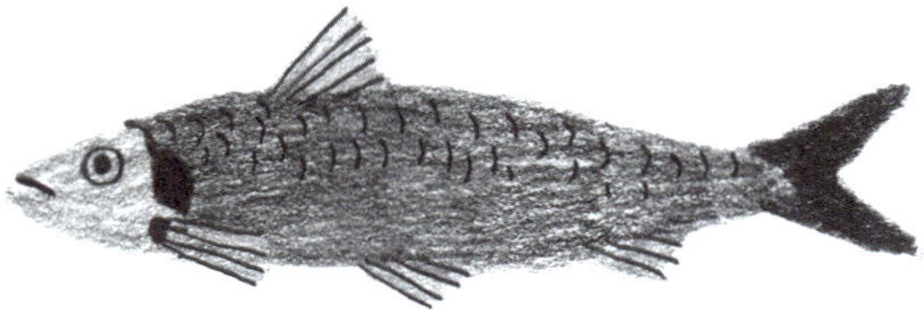

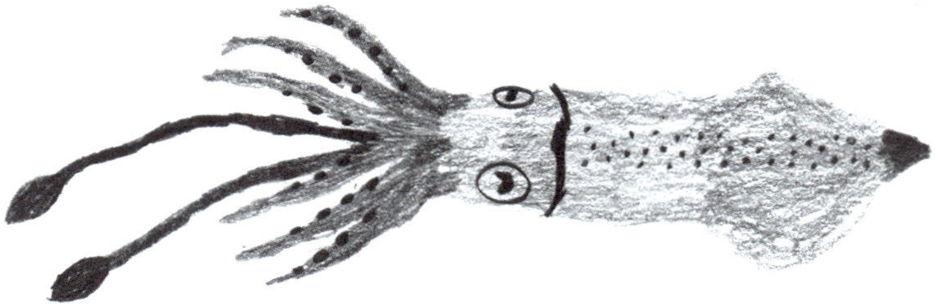

Toothed whales

Toothed whales are the smallest of the cetaceans. Most of them are closer to dolphins, the most famous member of the group, but others, such as the sperm and killer whales, are more easily compared to actual whales.
Have you ever heard the world *odontologist*? I'm talking about the dentist, the tooth doctor. If you think about it, it sounds like the word *odontoceti*, which is the systematic name for toothed whales and means "whale with **teeth**" in Greek. These whales eat larger animals, such as squid or fish of varying size. However, the teeth of these animals are not like our own, which are divided into different shapes suitable for different uses. They are all the same pointed shape. They are like mini harpoons which are used to seize the prey, which is then swallowed whole.

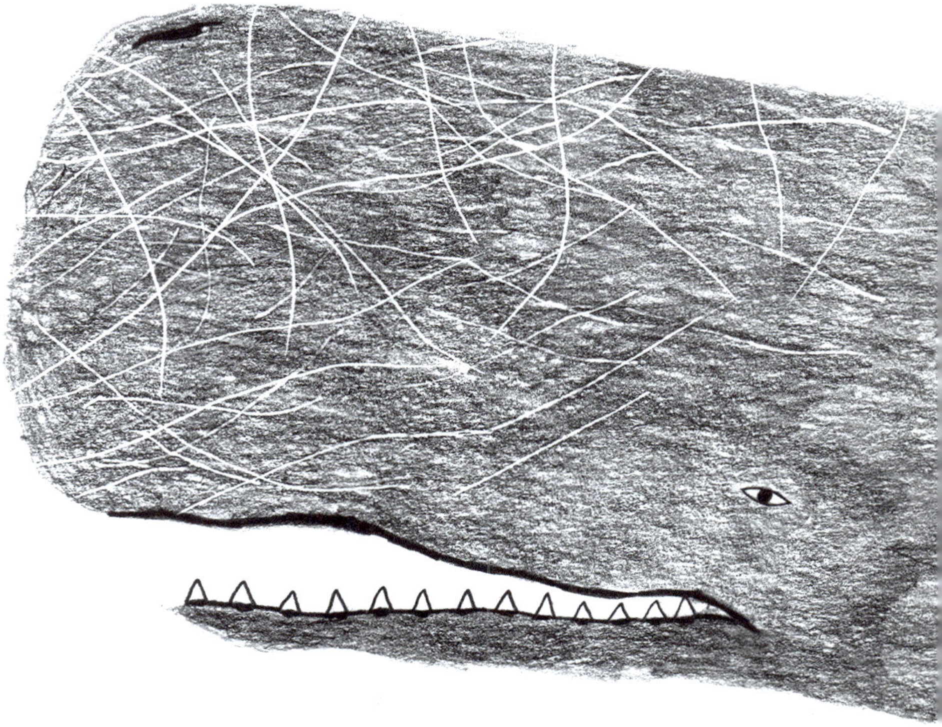

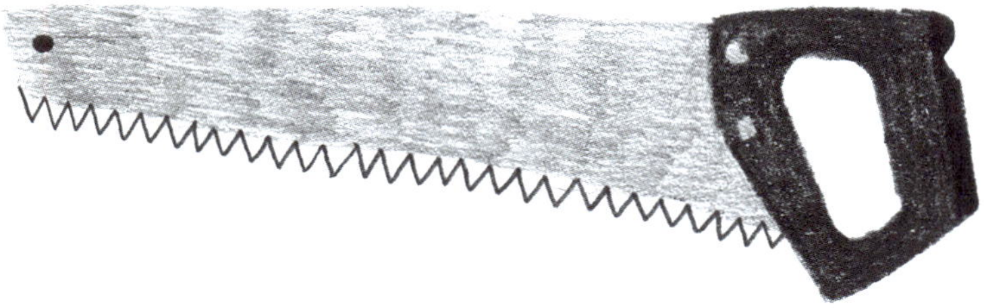

And now looking at the **toothed whale** teeth, you can't help but think of a saw!

A long time ago

Whales have not always been marine animals, this is the result of a long process of evolution! At first, they had legs and walked on land like other mammals.

The first **cetacean** that appeared on the face of the earth was the *pakicetus*, about 50 million years ago.

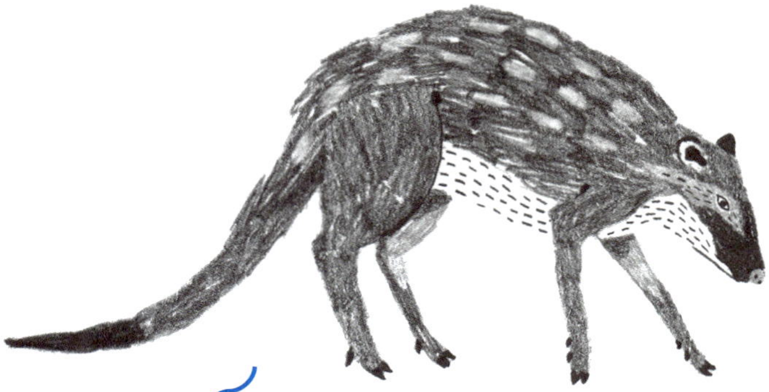

Indohyus
More than 50 million years ago
Length: 40-70 cm

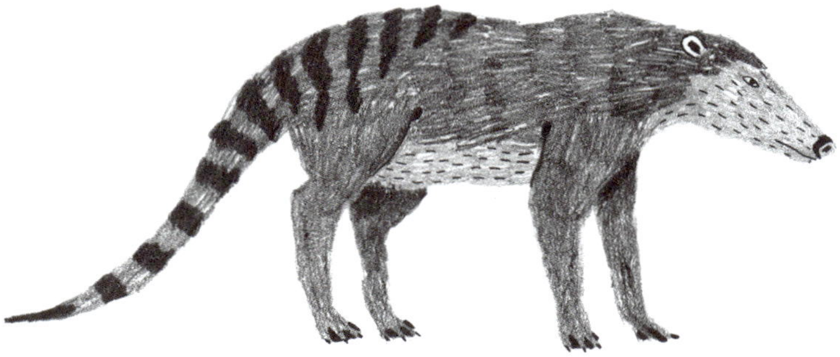

Pakicetus
55 million years ago
Length: 100-160 cm

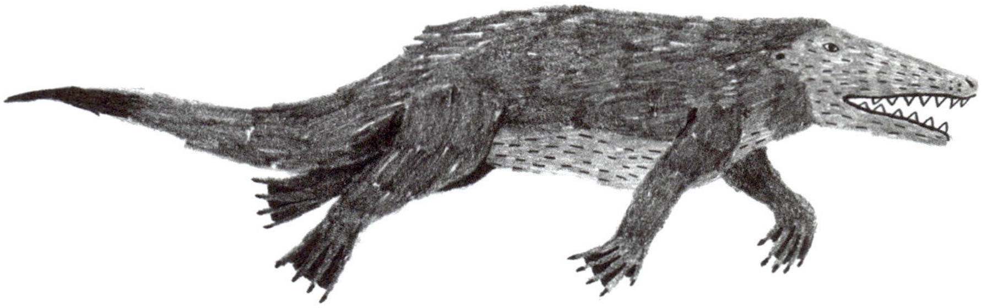

Ambulocetus
50-48 million years ago
Length: 3 metres

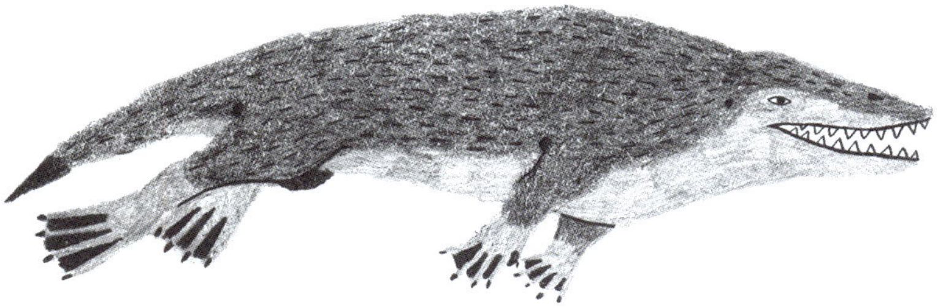

Rodhocetus
46-40 million years ago
Length: 3 metres

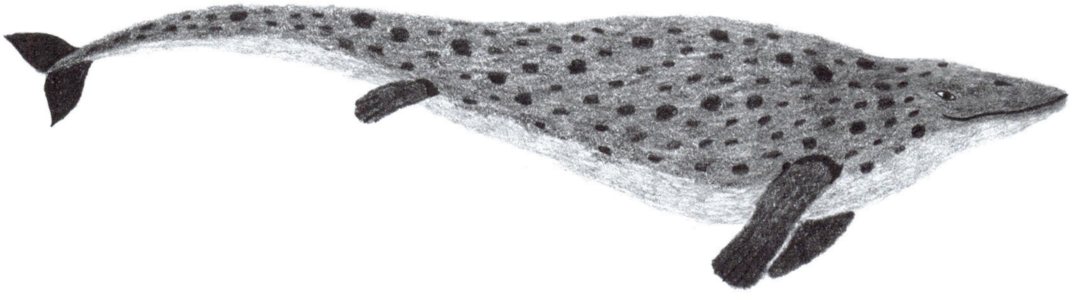

Primitive cetaceans are called **archaeoceti**. They were similar to mammals like **ungulates**, such as camels, cows, horses and, in particular, hippos. The transition from land to water was gradual. The hind legs gradually narrowed until they disappeared and a tail developed, as did the caudal fin which is ideal for swimming.

Dorudon
41-33 million years ago
Length: 5 metres

Nowadays

When we talk about **whales**, we often mean large cetaceans, but there are much fewer real whales than we imagine. Let me explain, baleen whales are divided into **three families**:

The whale family
Balaenidae
(Bowhead whale)

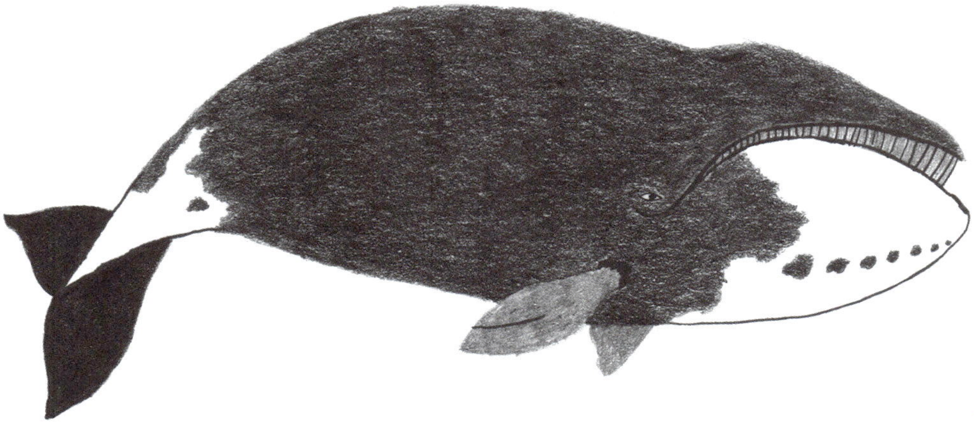

The rorqual family
Balaenopteridae
(Fin whale)

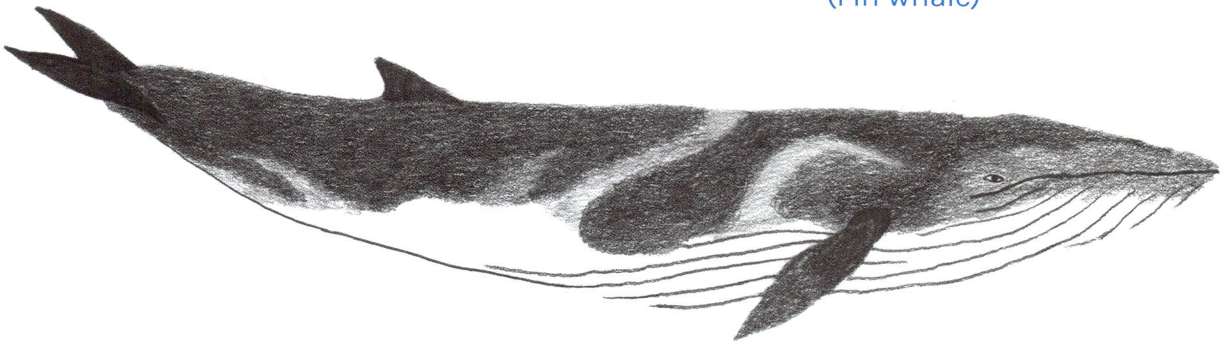

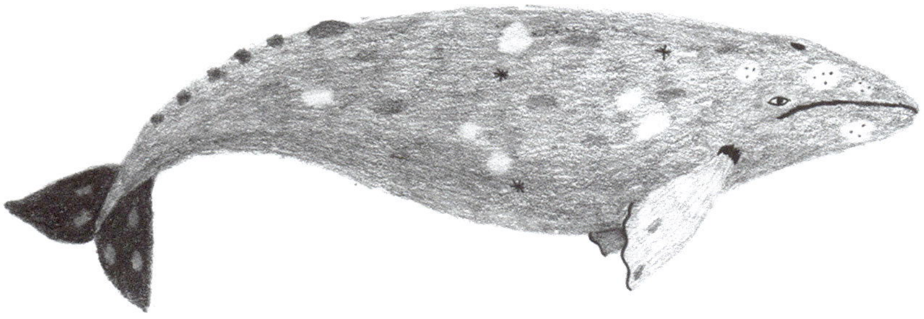

The eschrichtiidae family
Eschrichtiidae
(Grey whale)

Whales are the hardiest of all cetaceans,
and they are never in a hurry,
they are always swimming along,
slowly and peacefully.
They can be recognised by their head:
it is enormous, with a typical arch shape.
It is so big that it can sometimes make up
almost one third of the entire body.
The **baleen plates** are particularly long,
measuring up to three metres in length.

Fin whales have two qualities that make
them unique among baleen whales!
To start with, they have an extra fin
on their back, the **dorsal fin**.
As if that were not enough, they have **folds
of skin** on the underside of their body, which
allow them to widen their mouths and fill it
with as much food as they want. The long,
slender body is particularly hydrodynamic,
ideal for swimming at full speed. They are also
called *balaenopteridae*. This means "whale with
wings" in Greek, because of their very long
pectoral fins.

The **eschrichtiidae** family is very strange
indeed. It is made up of only one member,
the **grey whale**. If you look at it carefully,
it seems to be a mixture of a whale and
a rorqual whale. It has a **hump** that looks like
the rorquals' dorsal fins, and there are even
some small **folds of skin**.
It has the typical **curved profile** of the whale,
even if it is somewhat less pronounced.
The body is also halfway between the other
two families; the grey whale is thinner than
a whale, but more robust than a rorqual whale.

Who is bigger?

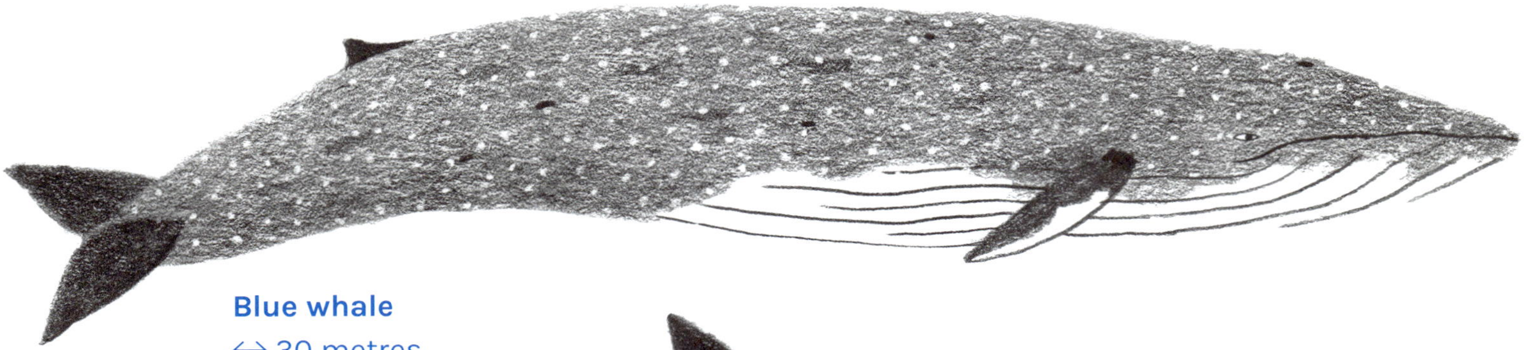

Blue whale
↔ 30 metres

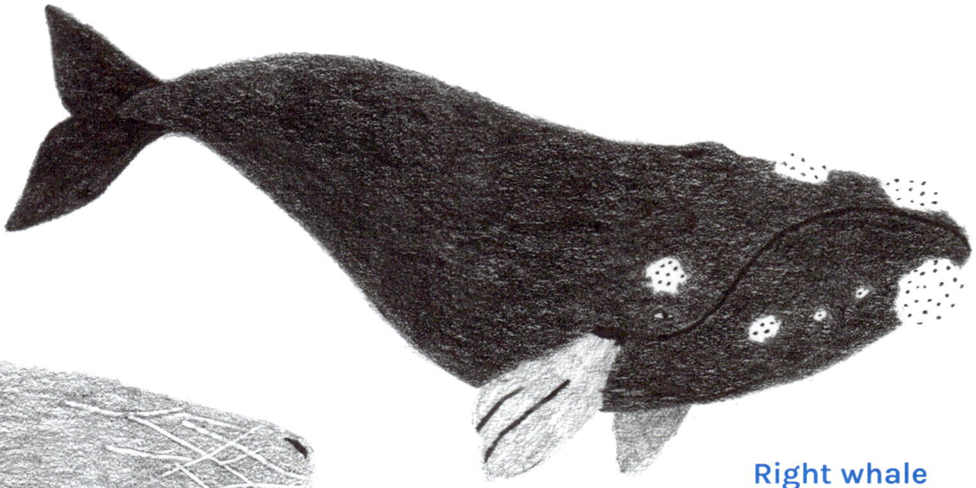

Right whale
↔ 18 metres

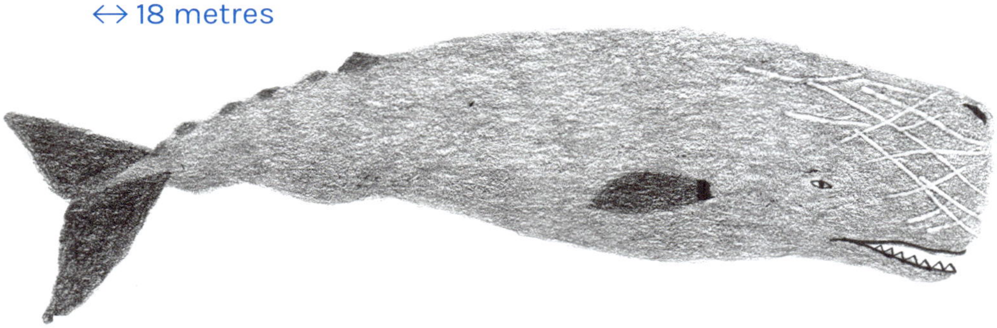

Sperm whale
↔ 18 metres

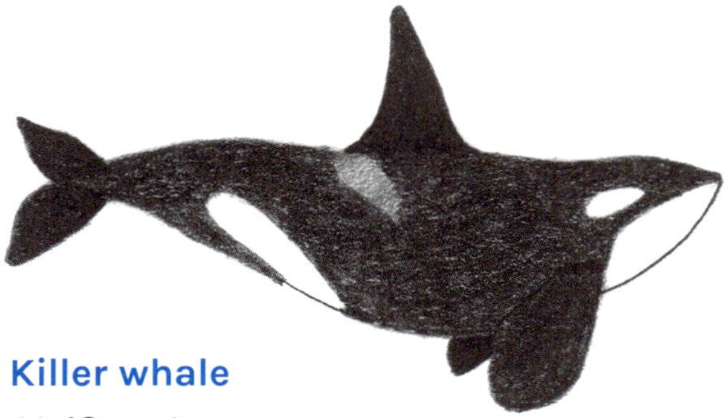

Killer whale
↔ 10 metres

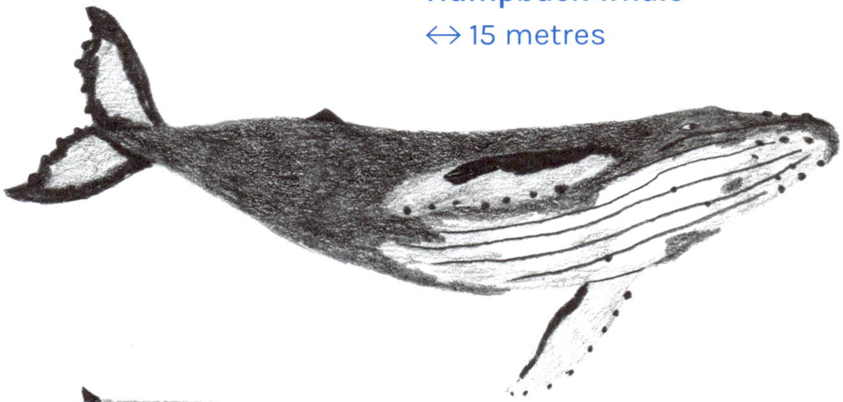

Humpback whale
↔ 15 metres

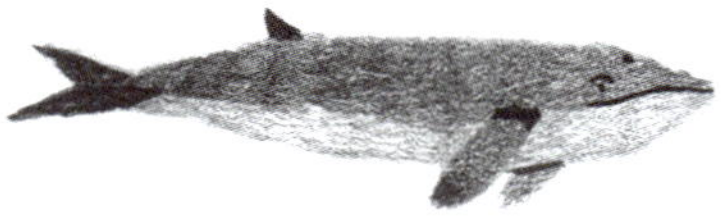

Pygmy right whale
↔ 6.5 metres

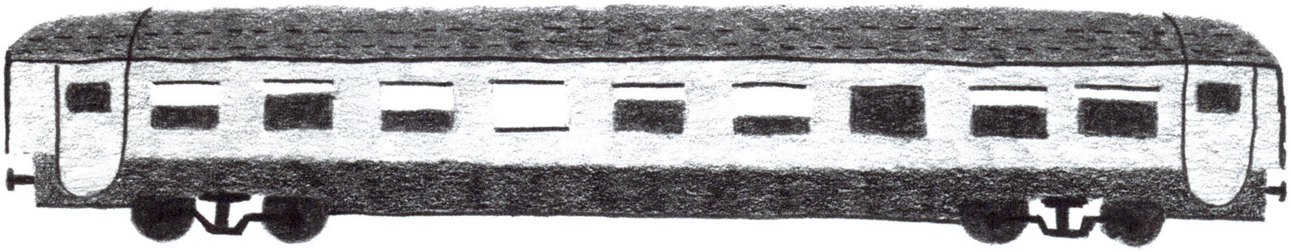

Train carriage
↔ 26 metres

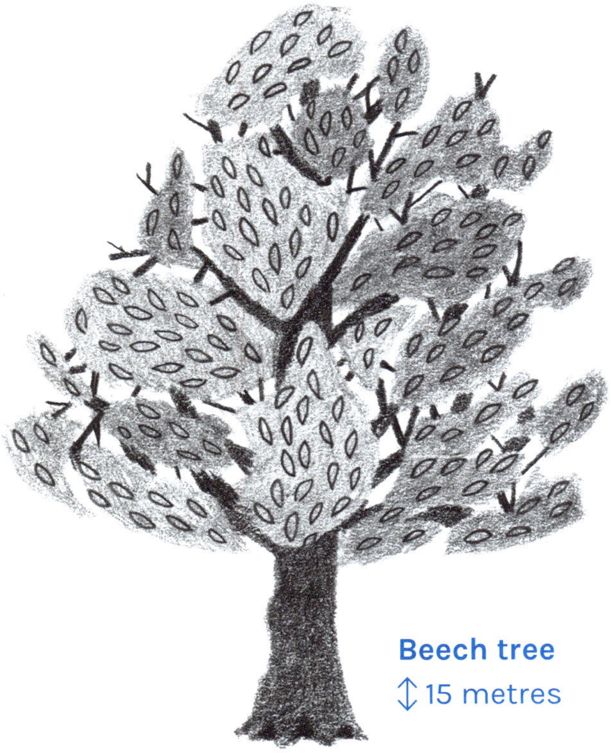

Beech tree
↕ 15 metres

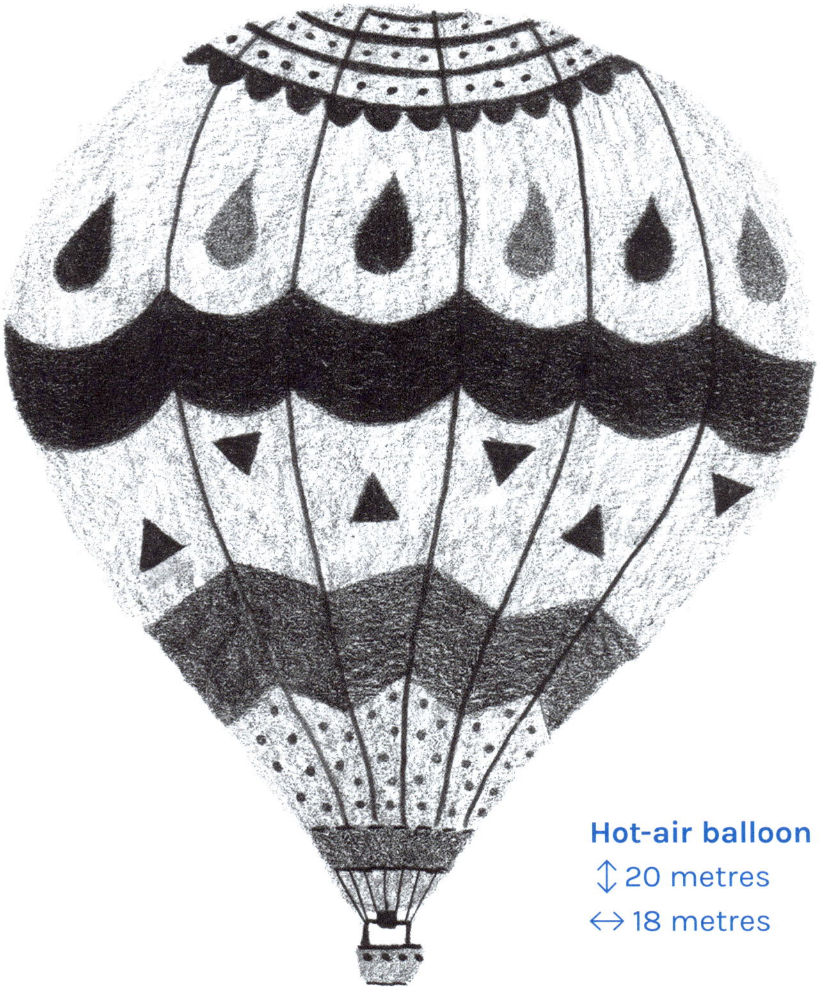

Hot-air balloon
↕ 20 metres
↔ 18 metres

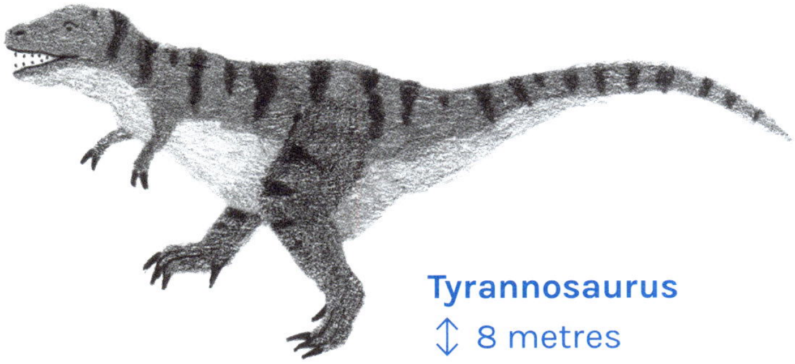

Tyrannosaurus
↕ 8 metres
↔ 13 metres

African elephant
↔ 6.5 metres

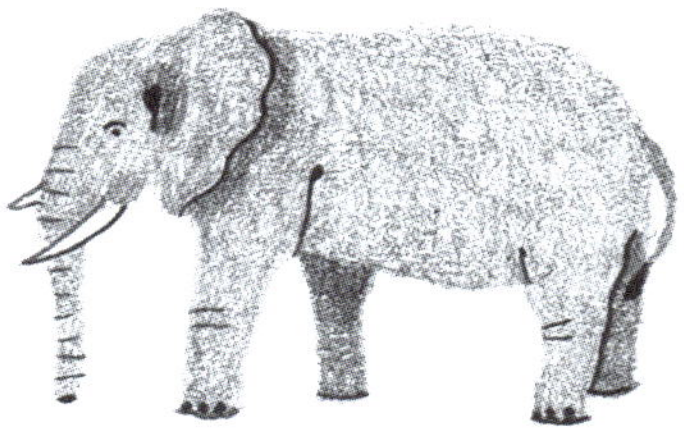

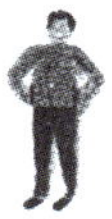

Human
↕ 1.70 metres

Water in the mouth

When whales eat, they need to make sure that they don't drink any seawater. That's not easy when you live in the sea! Luckily they have baleen plates, which they use to solve this problem.

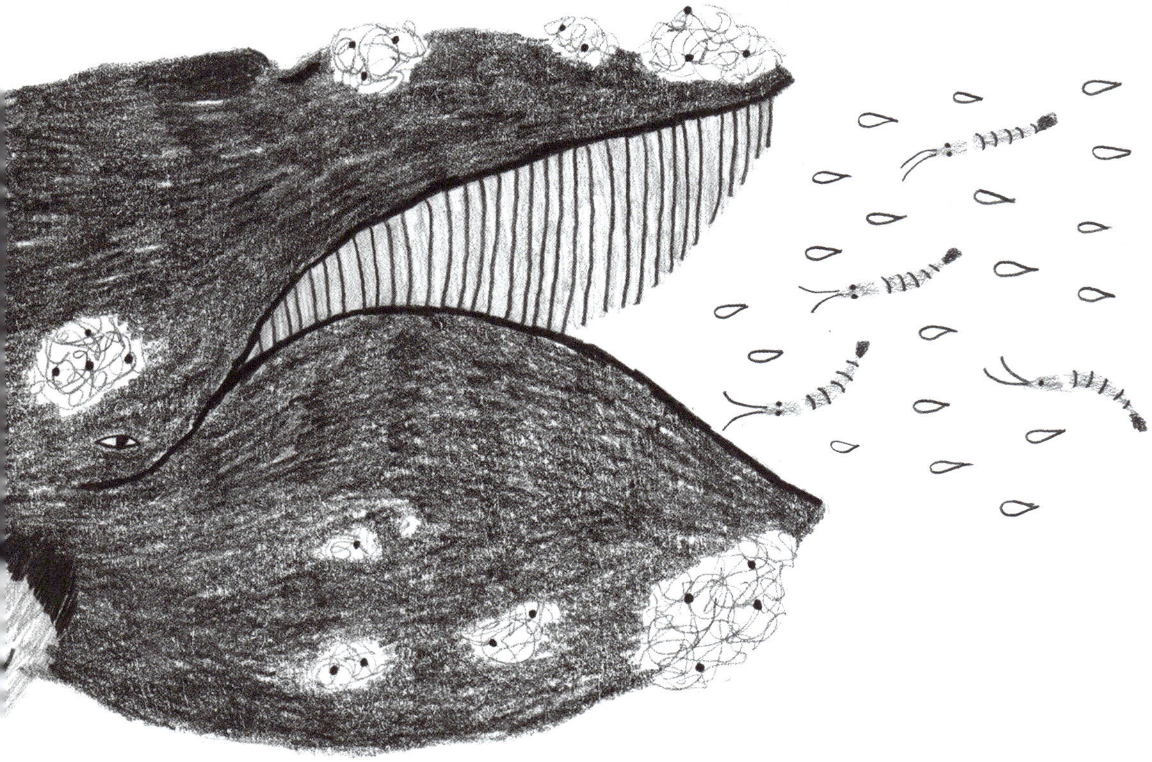

The first step is getting both **food** and **seawater** into the mouth.
Each whale has their own way of doing it.
Whales swim very **slowly** close to the surface. They are **constantly** eating, unlike rorquals. **Rorqual whales** are much **quicker** and they spring on their prey with an open mouth, swallowing a lot of seawater in addition to their food.

Once everything is in their mouth, they need to let out water without allowing their prey to escape! The dense structure of the **baleen plate** acts as a **filter**: whales push the water out **with their tongue**, pushing it through the plates. The captured krill and fish are too big to pass through, so they remain trapped inside the mouth.

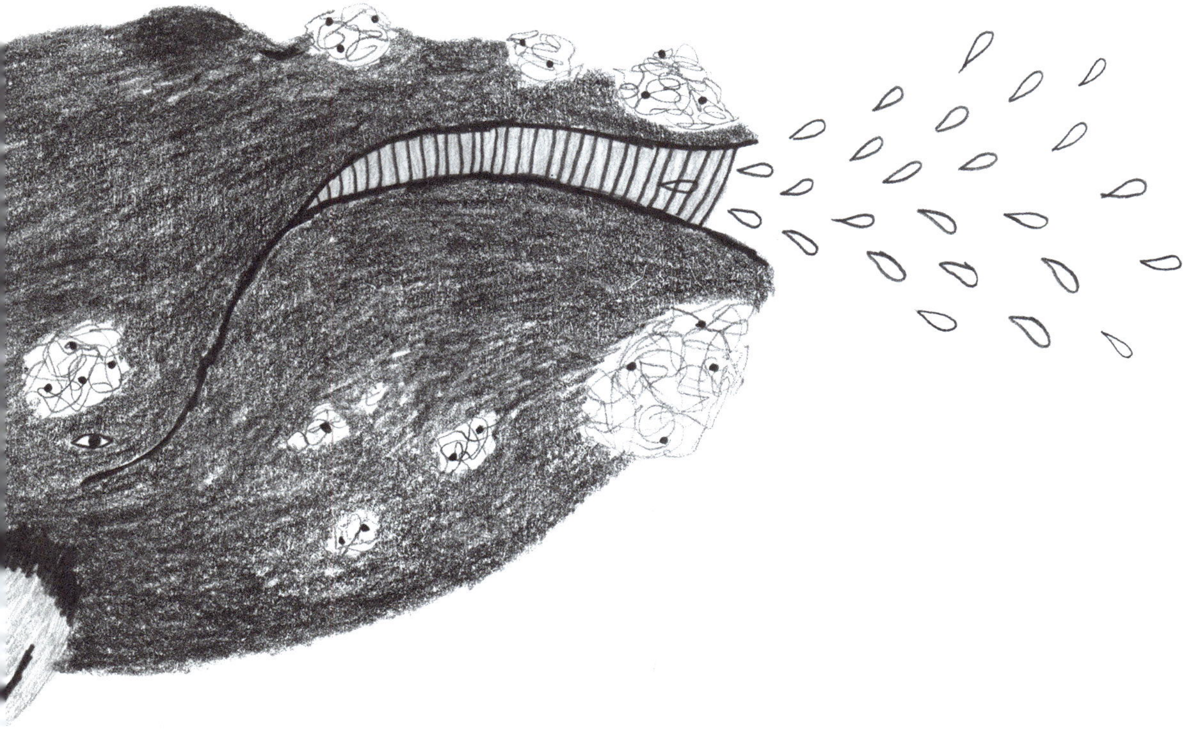

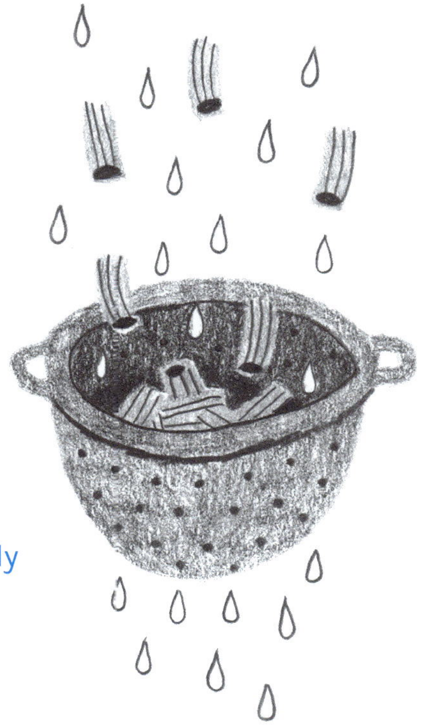

If you think about it, it works similarly to a colander. Both water and food enter, but the food remains after the water is drained away.

A constant mouthful

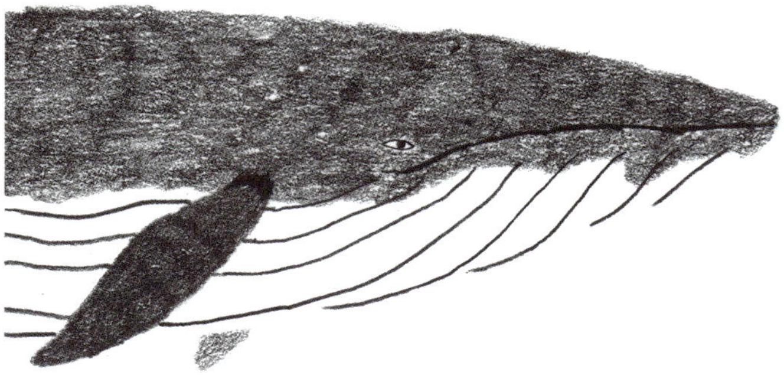

From the mouth down to the belly, underneath blue whales you see nothing but **folds of skin**. These special folds are relaxed to the extent that the mouth can be transformed into an extraordinarily spacious hollow, where there is no limit to the amount of fish that can enter. There is no "superpower" greater than this while hunting. Why chase after one fish at a time when you can swallow the whole school in one glup?

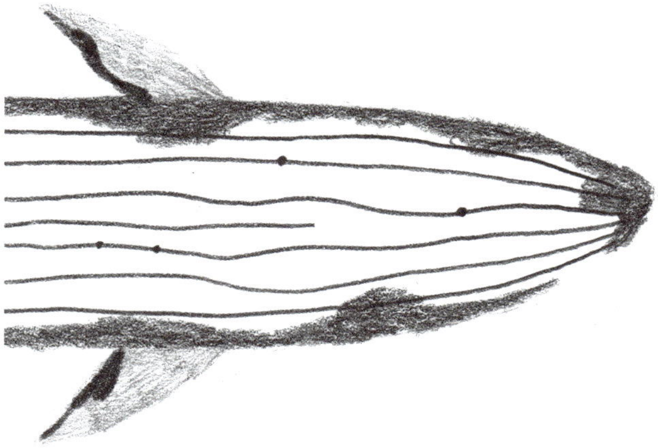

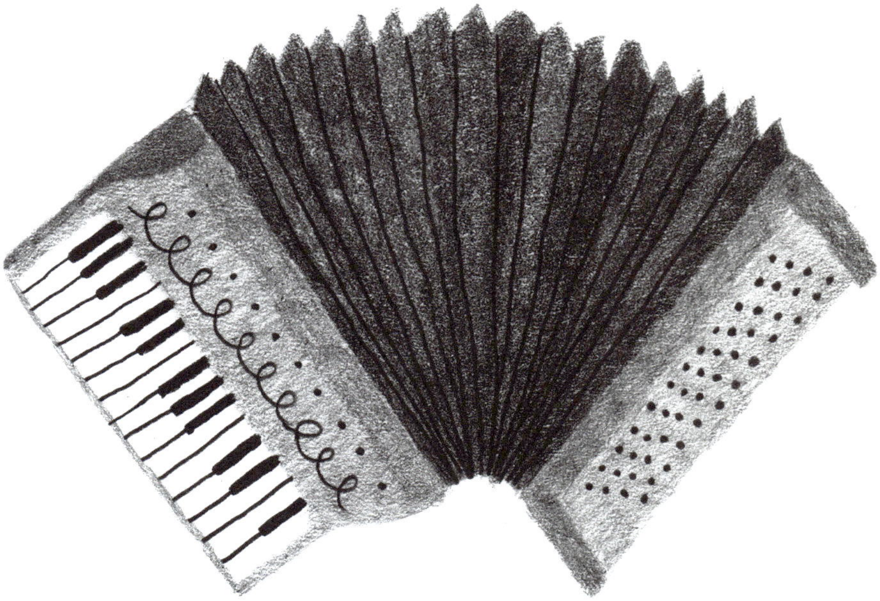

Have you ever seen an accordion? The central bellows on this instrument work and expand in exactly the same way as the blue whale's belly!

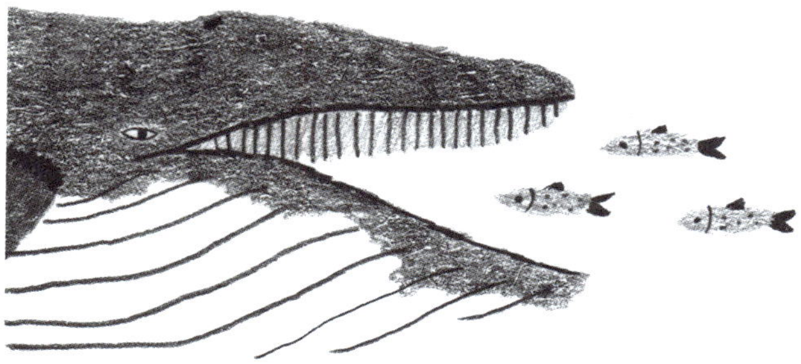

This is just the beginning...

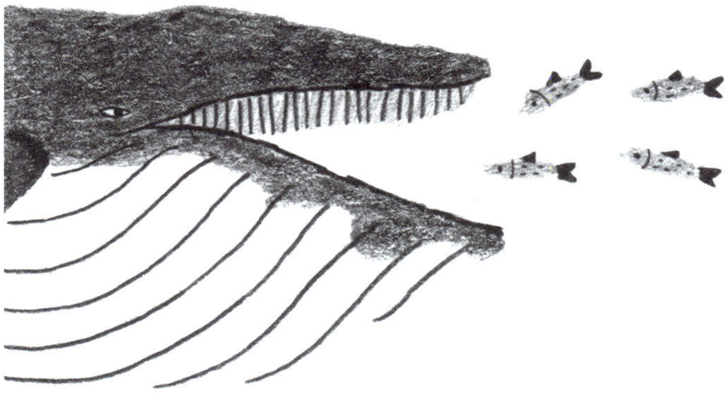

We're not even halfway there!

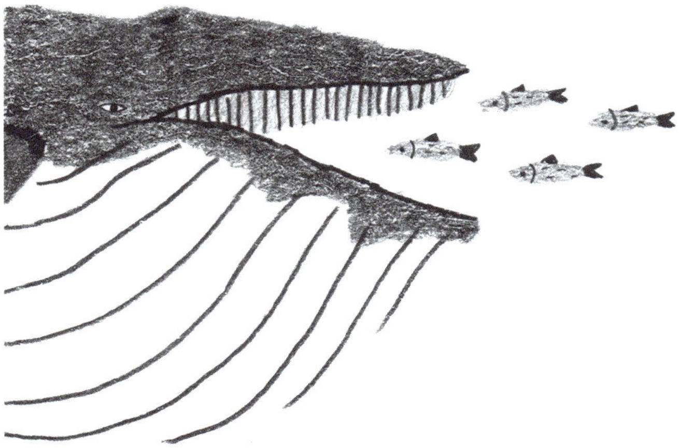

There's still a hole to be filled...

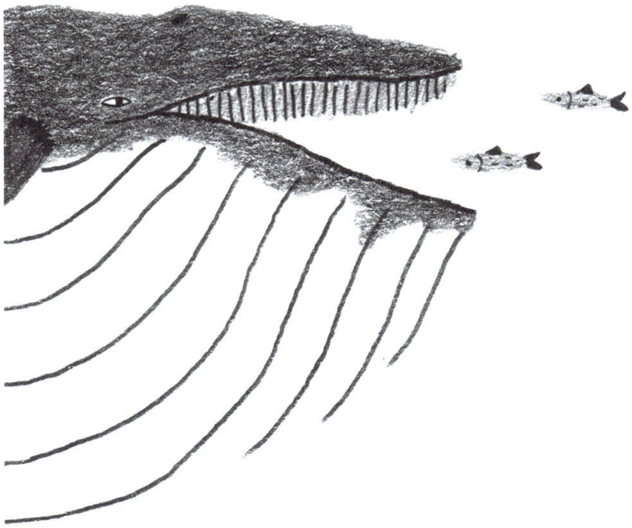

The last two, I promise!

A blue whale can hold up to a third of its entire body weight of food and water in its mouth. So if a blue whale weighs around 180 tonnes, it could even hold a 60 tonne tank in its mouth!

Enjoy your meal

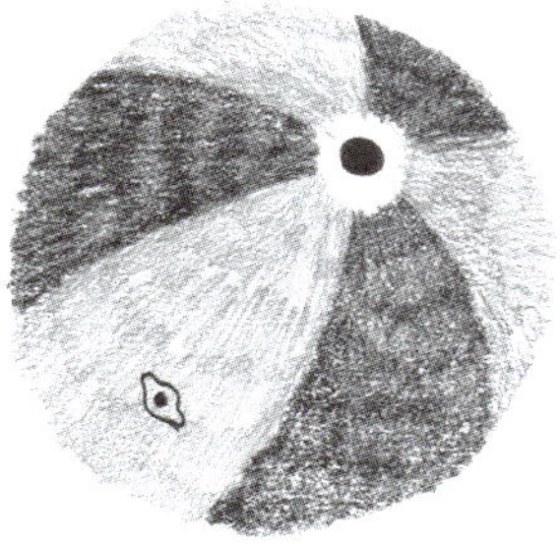

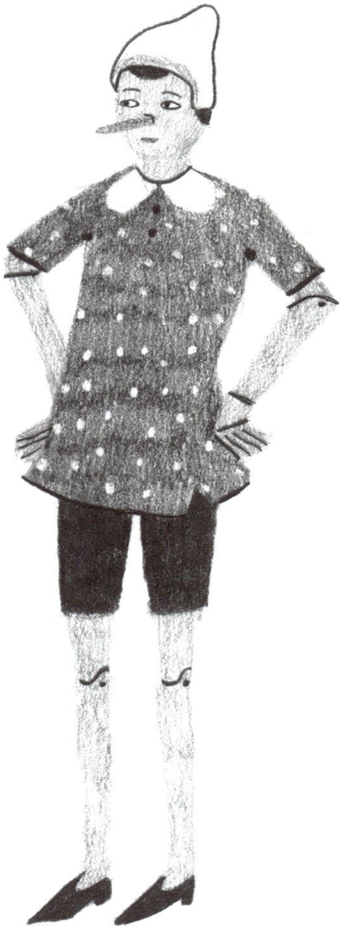

Did a whale eat Pinocchio?!
You're getting confused, that was a dogfish shark! Whales don't eat humans, let alone puppets! It's not that they don't like them, they just aren't able to.

Whales don't chew their food, they swallow it whole. Before reaching the stomach, the food passes through the pharynx which, in larger whales, is about the size of a beach ball. Even the thinnest human wouldn't pass through it!

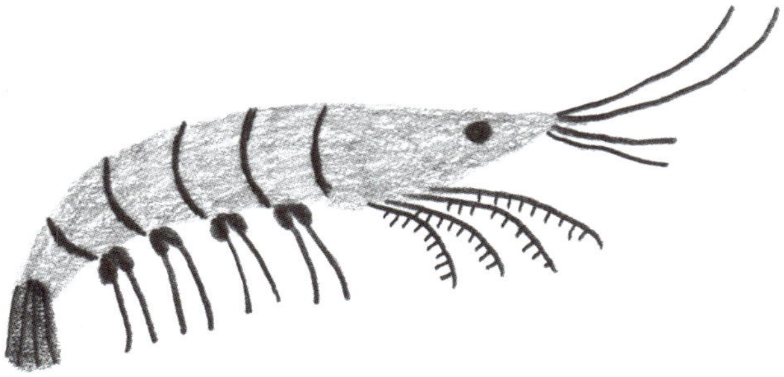

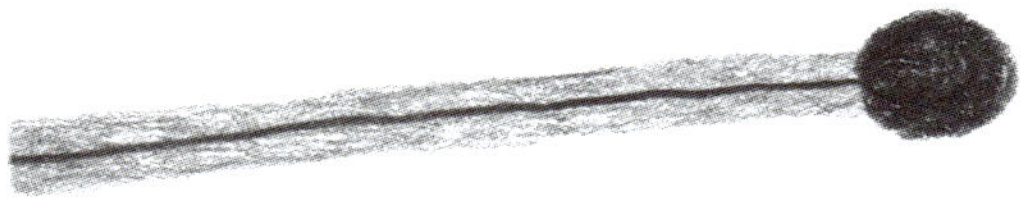

So how do they satisfy their appetite?
If they can't eat big things, then the alternative is to eat lots of small things! A whale's favourite fool is **krill**, a crustacean that is about as big as a matchstick. The sea is full of these little creatures and blue whales are well aware of this, eating up to 40 million krill each day.

Cetaceans have **three stomachs**, where food is digested.

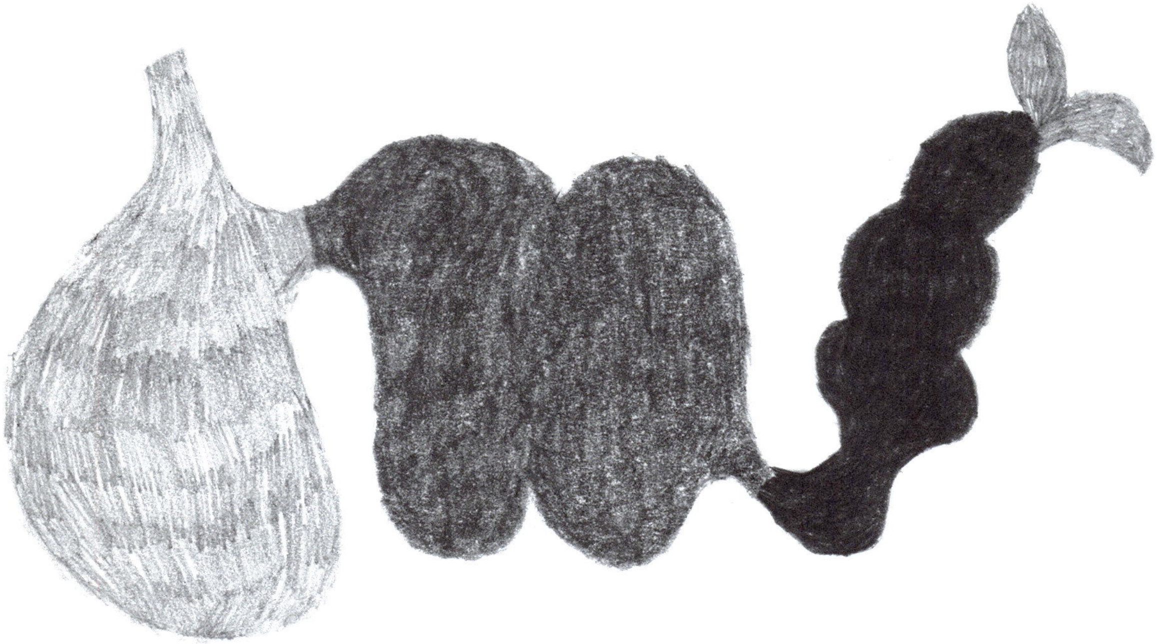

The **first stomach** performs a similar function to our chewing. It is equipped with "teeth" and when it contracts, food is broken down.

In the **second stomach**, which is the main one, there are a number of different glands that release gastric fluids, which cause food to dissolve.

Digestion ends in the **third stomach**, where food passes into the intestine and the nutrients are absorbed.

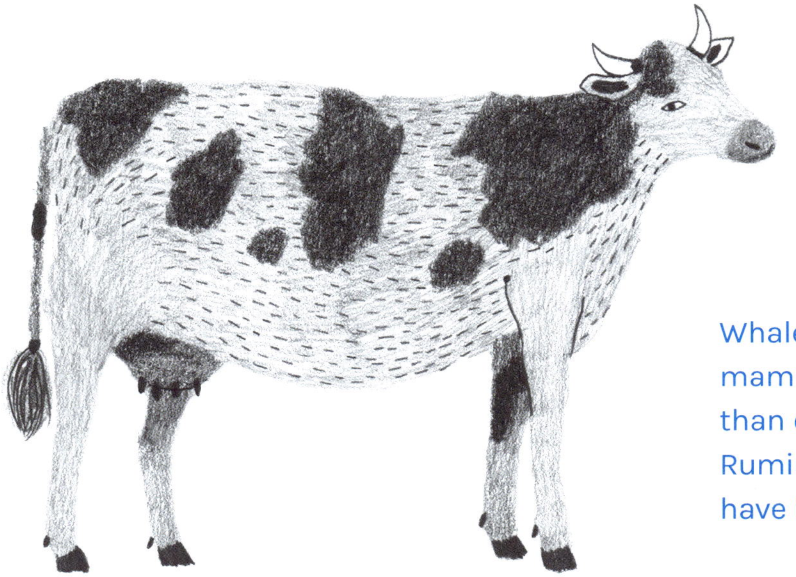

Whales are not the only mammals to have more than one stomach. Ruminants, like cows, have four!

Upturned nose

I bet you have been taught how to swim underwater. When you dive down, you normally take a deep breath and hold it until you get back to the surface to get some air. Whales do the same thing, only they can hold their breath for much longer. Sperm whales can do it for two hours.

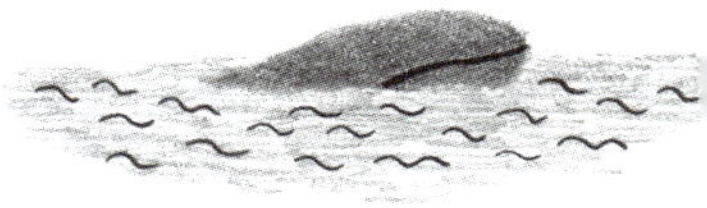

Your nose is in the middle of your face, but a whale's nose is on top of its head and it's called a **blowhole**.

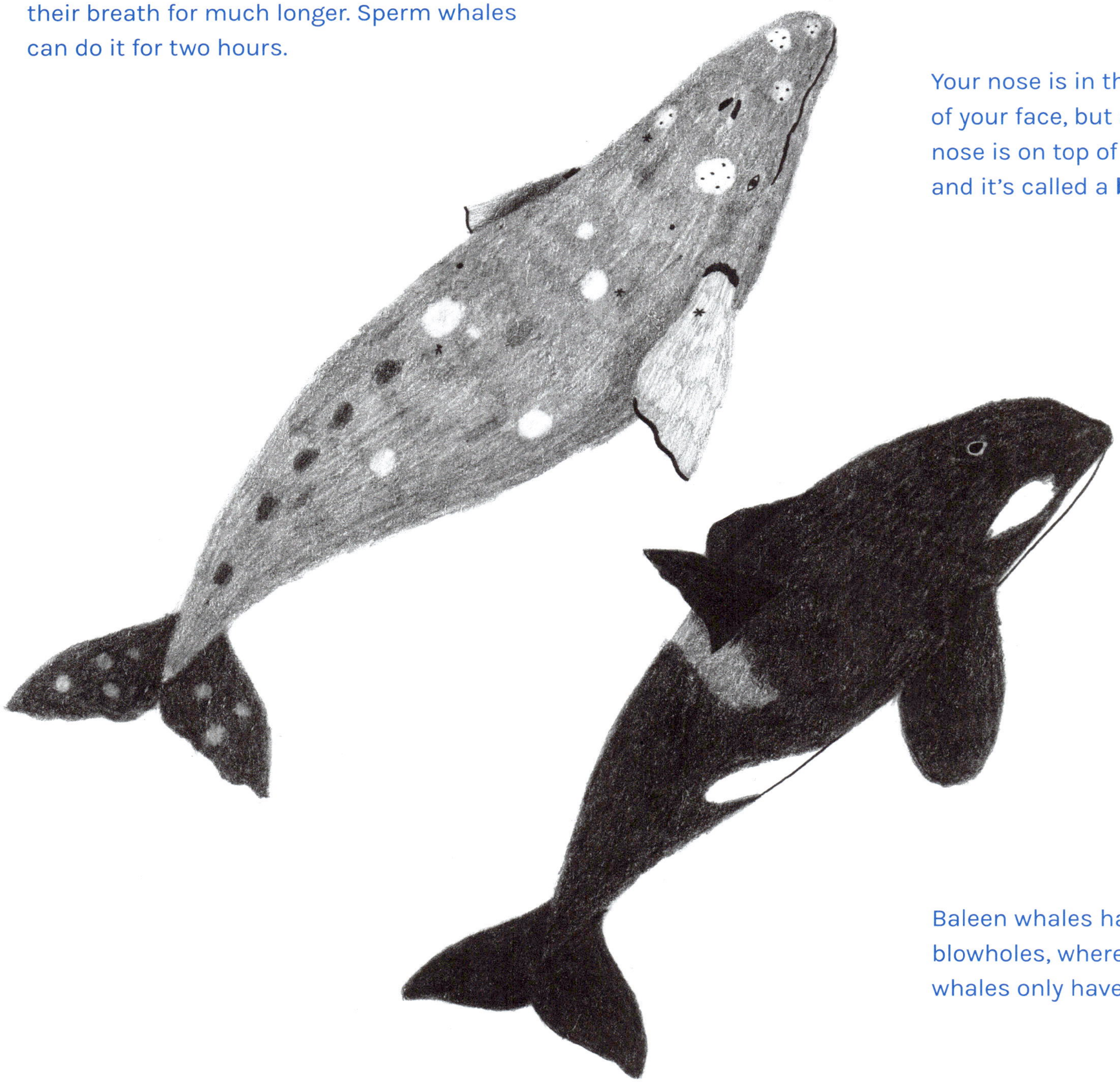

Baleen whales have two blowholes, whereas toothed whales only have one.

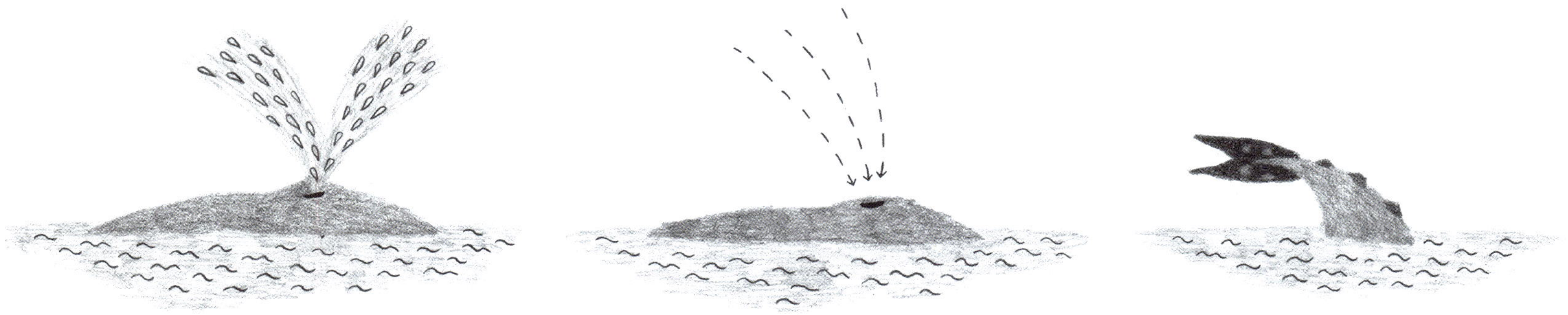

When whales come up to breathe, they rise in a vertical arc on the surface of the water. The blowhole opens and they **exhale**, releasing the **blow** that is typical of whales. They **breathe in** immediately, gathering up the necessary oxygen to dive down again.

When they sleep, whales remain close to the surface in order to breathe. Some like to even keep their blowhole out of the water while sleeping. Humans breathe involuntarily but that is not the case with whales. Even when they sleep, they must remain conscious.

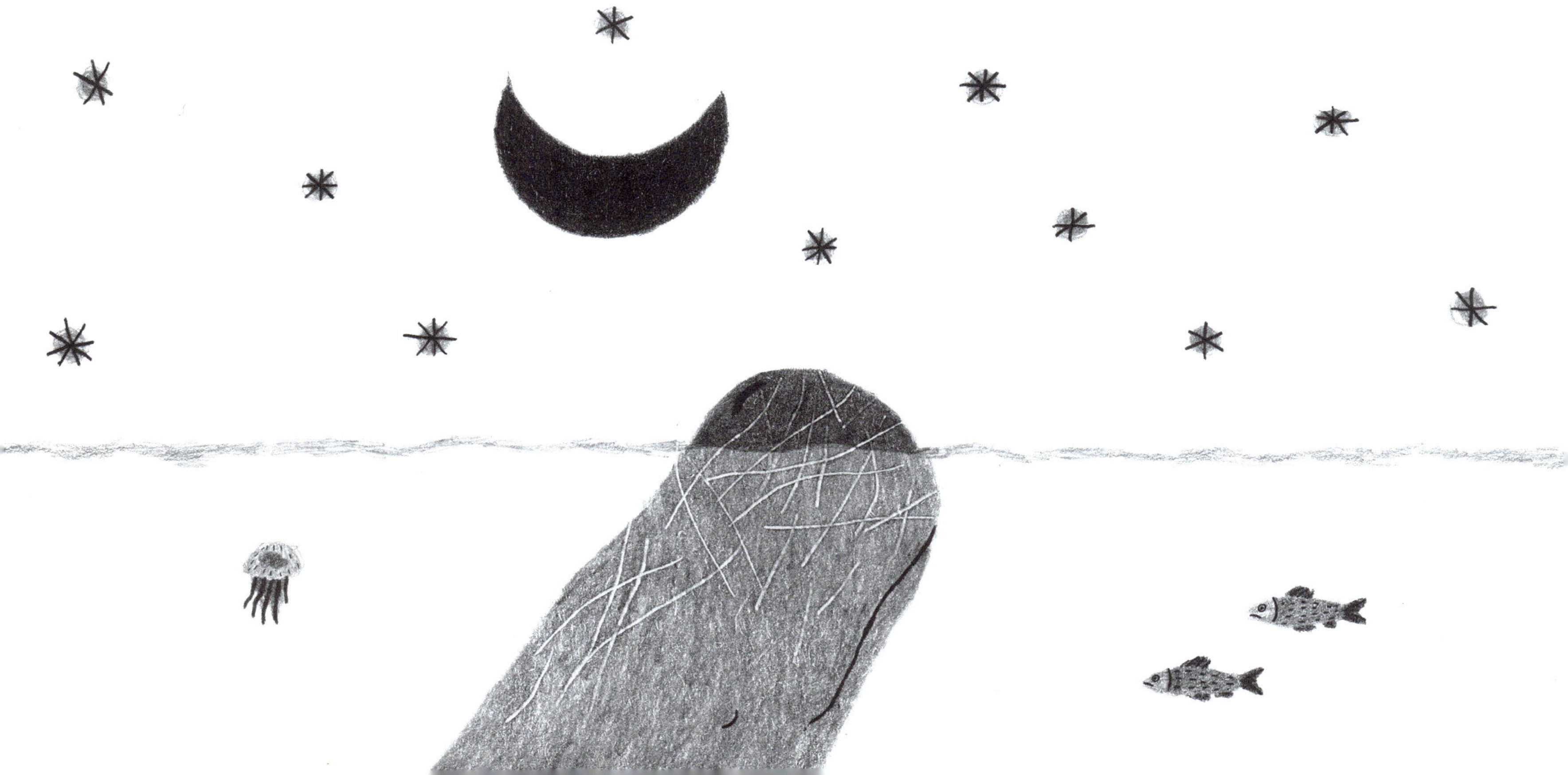

Watch out for splashes

Blue whale
Thin and straight,
this whale's blow takes
first prize with
a height of **9 metres**.

Bowhead whale
This V-shaped blow divides
into two halves that reach
7 metres.

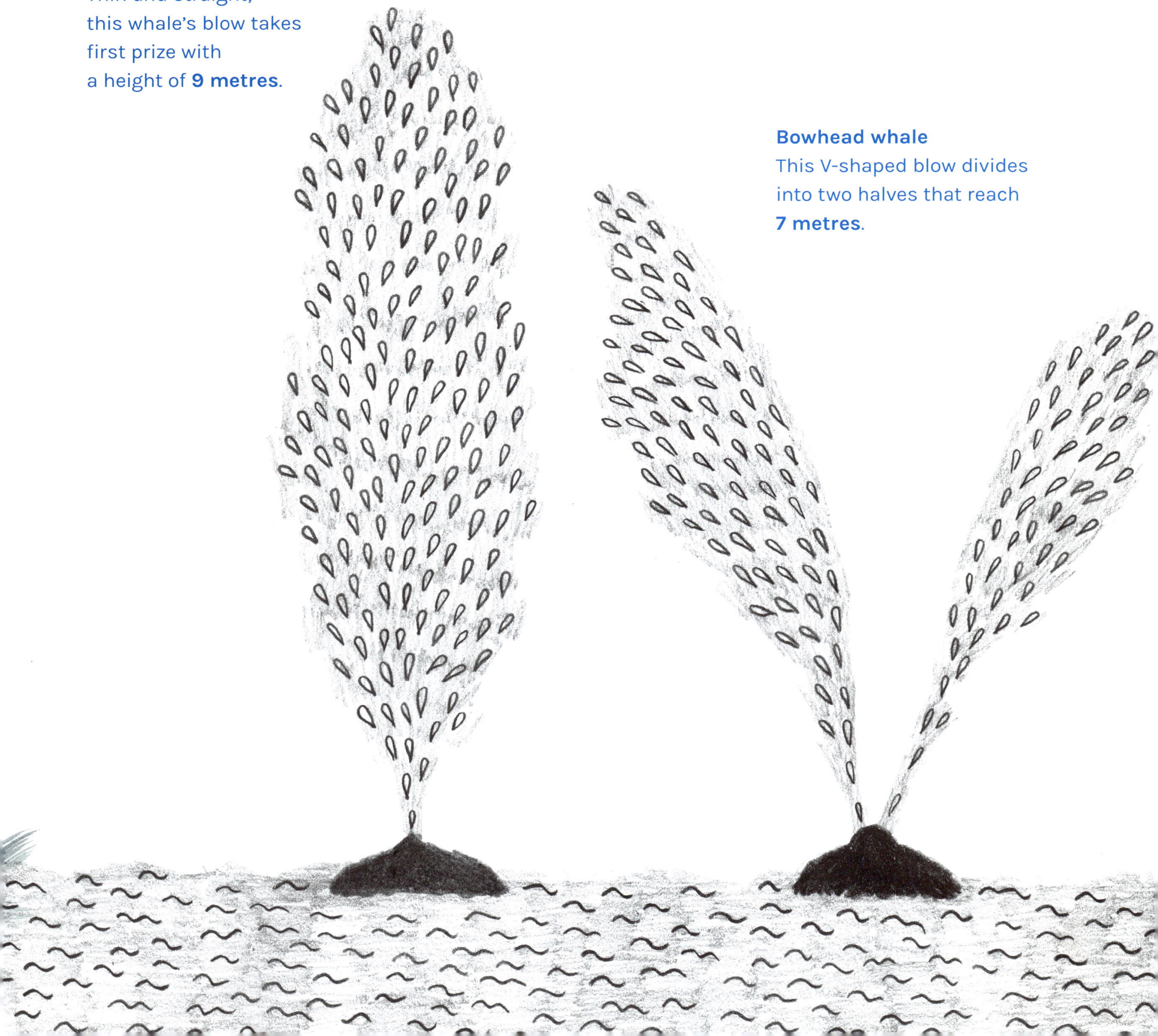

When a whale emerges from the water to breathe, it looks like a huge jet of water comes out of the blowhole. What really comes out is mostly air, and it is known as the **blow**. It's important to be able to distinguish the blows of marine mammals!
It's also important to distinguish between the blows of different whales. Even for experts, who are often excellent swimmers, it is difficult to see them underwater so they need to be able to recognise the parts that can be seen above water.
And how can you fail to notice a blow that can reach the height of a three-storey building, or even taller?
Each whale has its own type of blow, and it can be recognised by its momentum, shape and power.

But what is blow made from?
It is a mixture of air, water vapour and droplets of oil and mucus contained within the body of the whale.

Humpback whale
This blow is different because it is usually wider than it is long. It reaches **3 metres** in height.

Sperm whale
The blow of a sperm whale is instantly recognisable, it is projected forwards and rises up to **2 metres**.

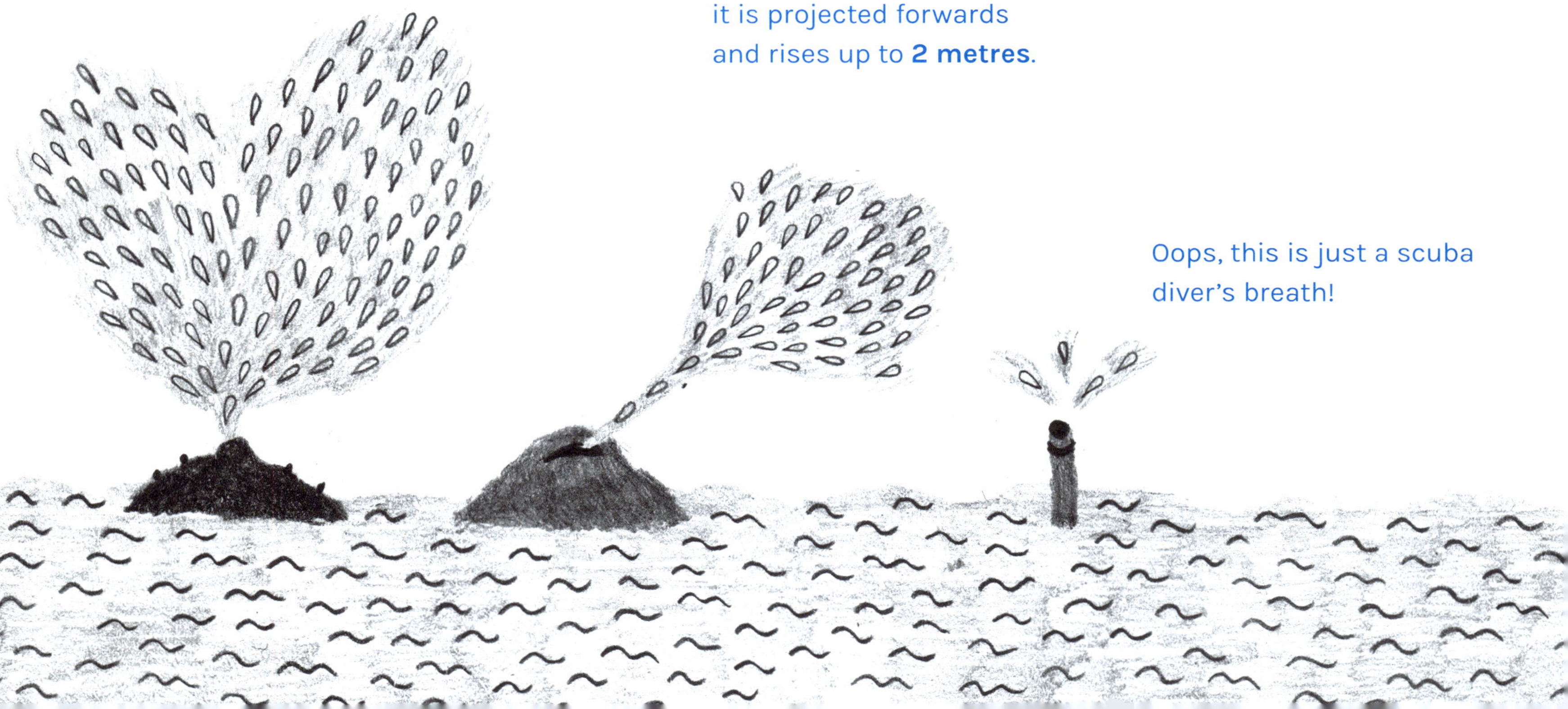

Oops, this is just a scuba diver's breath!

Born acrobats

Oh yes, whales are born acrobats. They jump, splash and flip over on themselves.
But what are their best stunts?

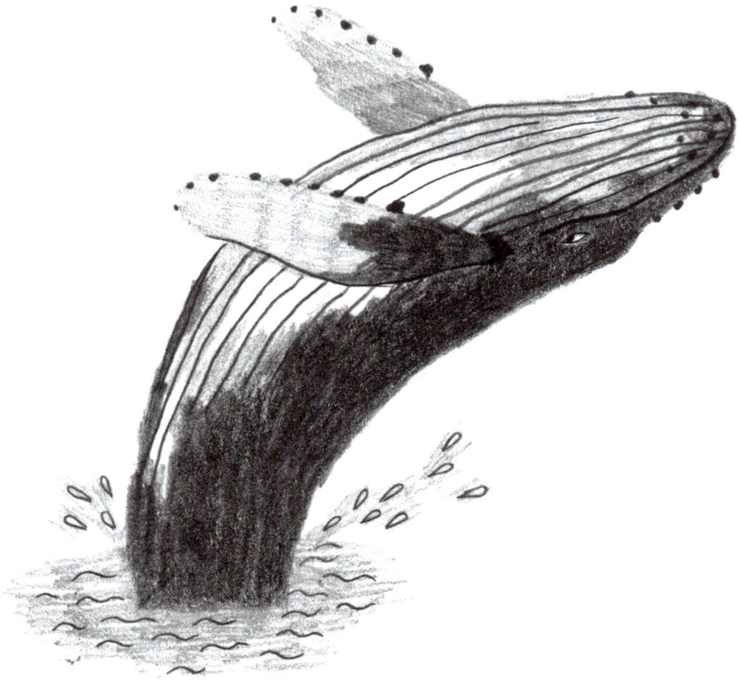

Breaching
Make sure you don't miss it because **breaching** is the only way you'll be able to see an entire whale! This is when it jumps completely out of the water, falling on its back or belly, twisting around completely.
The cause of this behaviour is not yet known. Some say that it is for courtship or challenge between whales. Others think it is a way to get rid of parasites. But it's probably just a way for them to play.

Lobtailing
If you can see a whale's tail rise up out of the water, be careful. You might be in line for a **slap**! **Lobtailing** is when a whale lifts its tail out of the water and smacks the surface. It is said to be an intimidating gesture or, because of the loud noise it makes, a form of communicating with the rest of the pod.

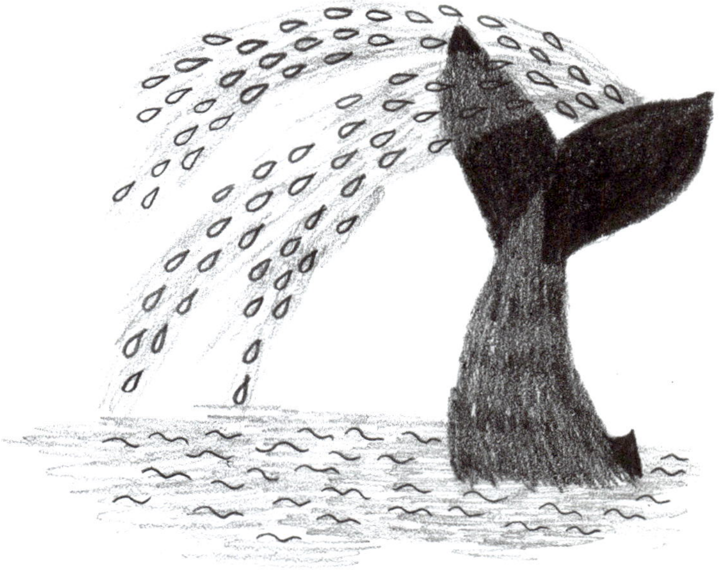

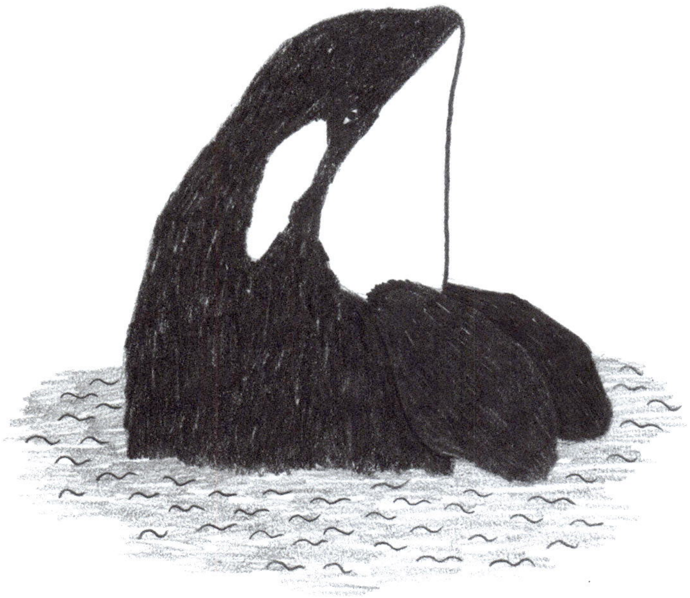

Spyhopping
"Who goes there?!"
Looking right, looking left: **spyhopping** is the name for a whale popping its head out of the water to see what's going on up there.

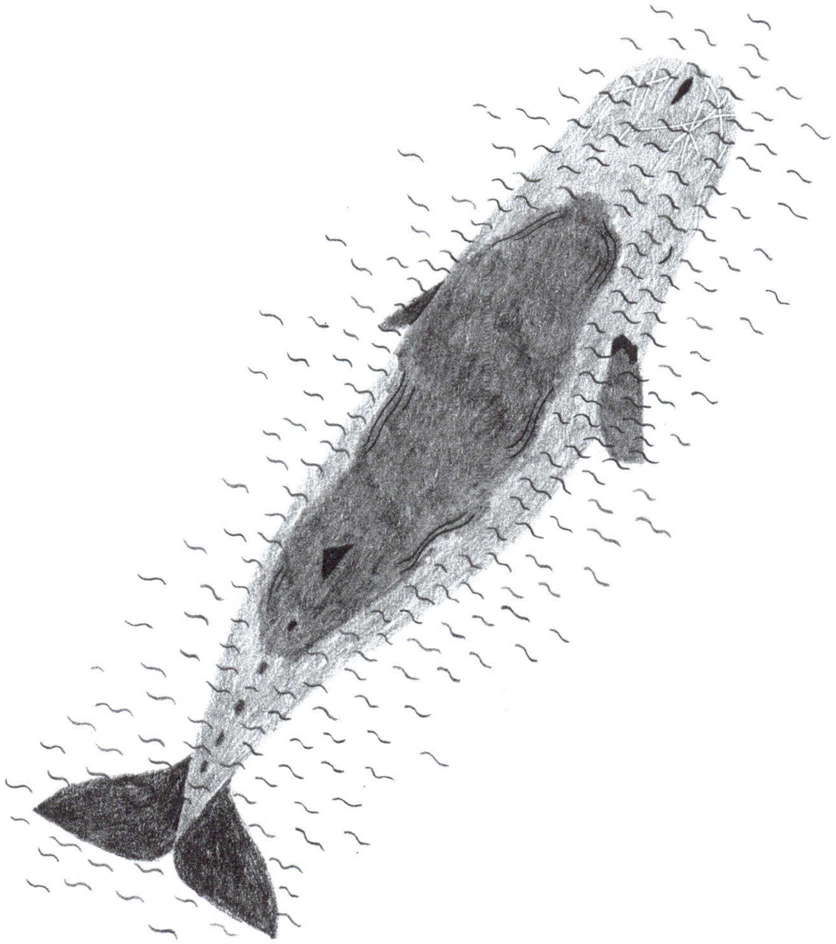

Logging
You get tired performing all of these tricks! After a day of leaping, you need to rest a little, floating on the seabed, as straight as a **tree trunk**. **Logging** is generally a group activity, with all of the whales in a pod relaxing, "stretched out" in the same direction.

Top qualities

Echolocation
It's not always easy to see where you're going underwater, even if you have a good view. This is why whales, and particularly toothed whales, have developed a sixth sense that helps them get around. They manage to "see" thanks to the **echo** caused by every single sound. This is how cetaceans communicate: the sounds they emit bounce off the closest obstacle, and head back towards the whale. It can be hard for us to imagine, but echoes allow whales to orient themselves in the darkest depths and to locate their prey, reconstructing their images. Do you know how a ship's radar works? Well this works in exactly the same way.

Language
Like us humans, whales can also "talk" by making sounds that have meanings to other whales. Whales can make a great variety of different sounds, each of them associated to a different action or a specific situation. It has even been proven that there are a number of "**dialects**" between members of the same species that change from group to group.

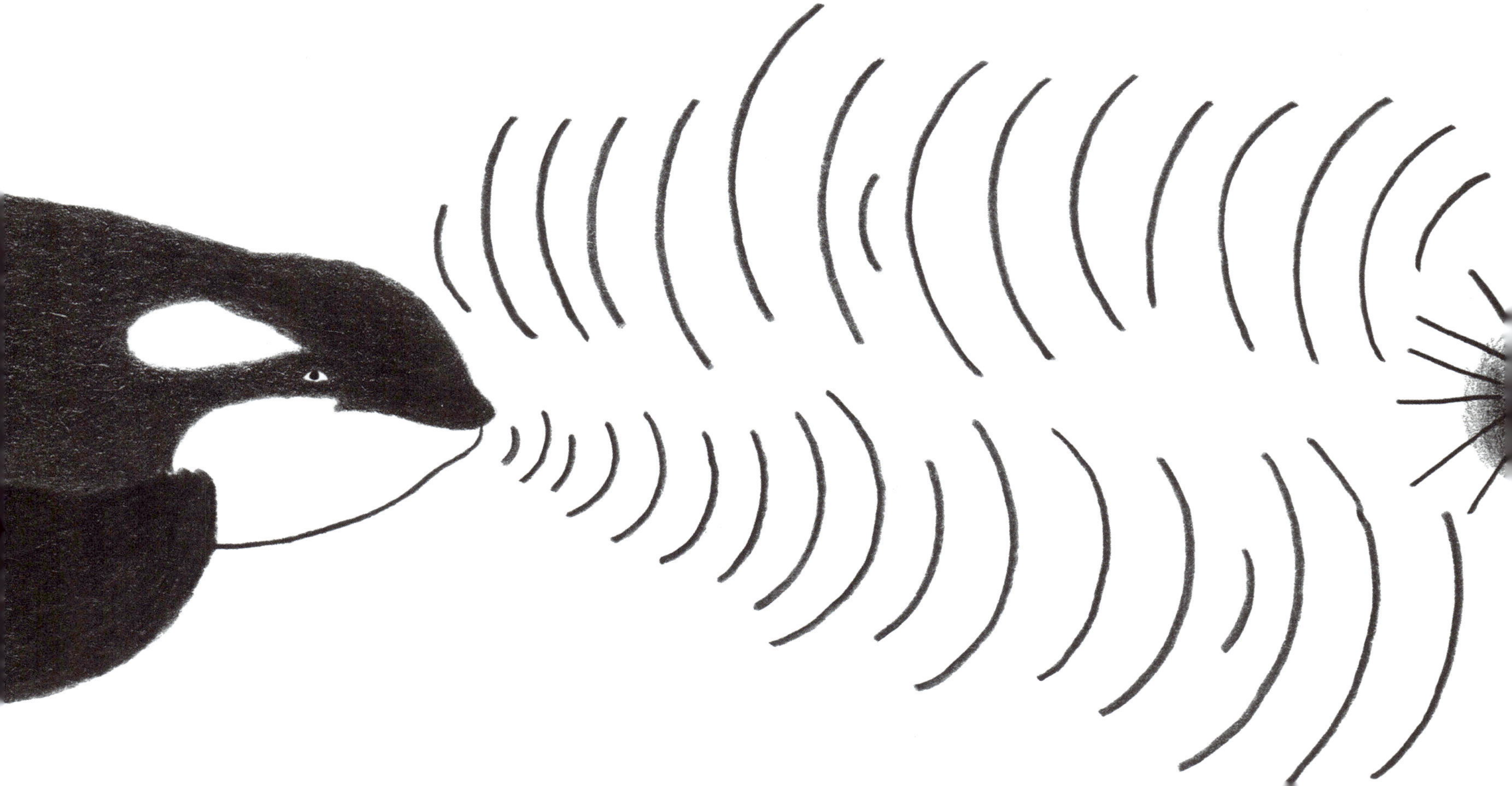

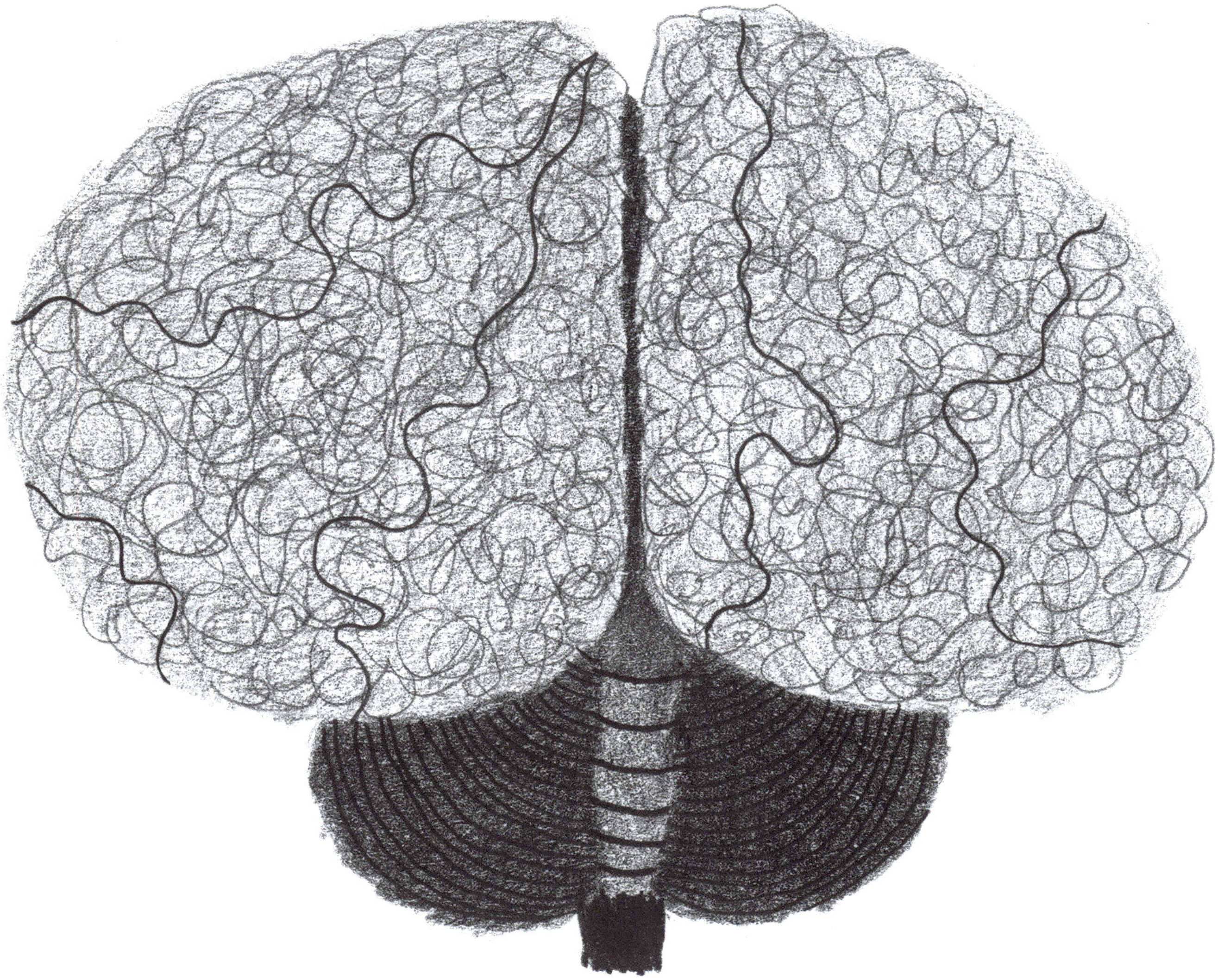

Intelligence

A whale's brain is, in some respects, very similar to a human brain. Is their **intelligence** similar to ours?
Many argue that their cleverness is due to the size of their brain, obviously in relation to the immense size of the whole body.
But instead of just looking at the brain, it is important to look at how whales behave.
Much of their behaviour is complex enough to be a true test of their intelligence.
They are **quick learners**, and their knowledge is passed down between "family members".
Each cetacean also invents its own strategies, especially during hunting and defending members of its own pod.

Around the world

In which city do you live?
If you were to ask the same question to whales, they wouldn't be able to give you an answer.
They are constantly on the move! They migrate throughout the entire year, in **winter** and **summer**, from the south to the north and from the north to the south.

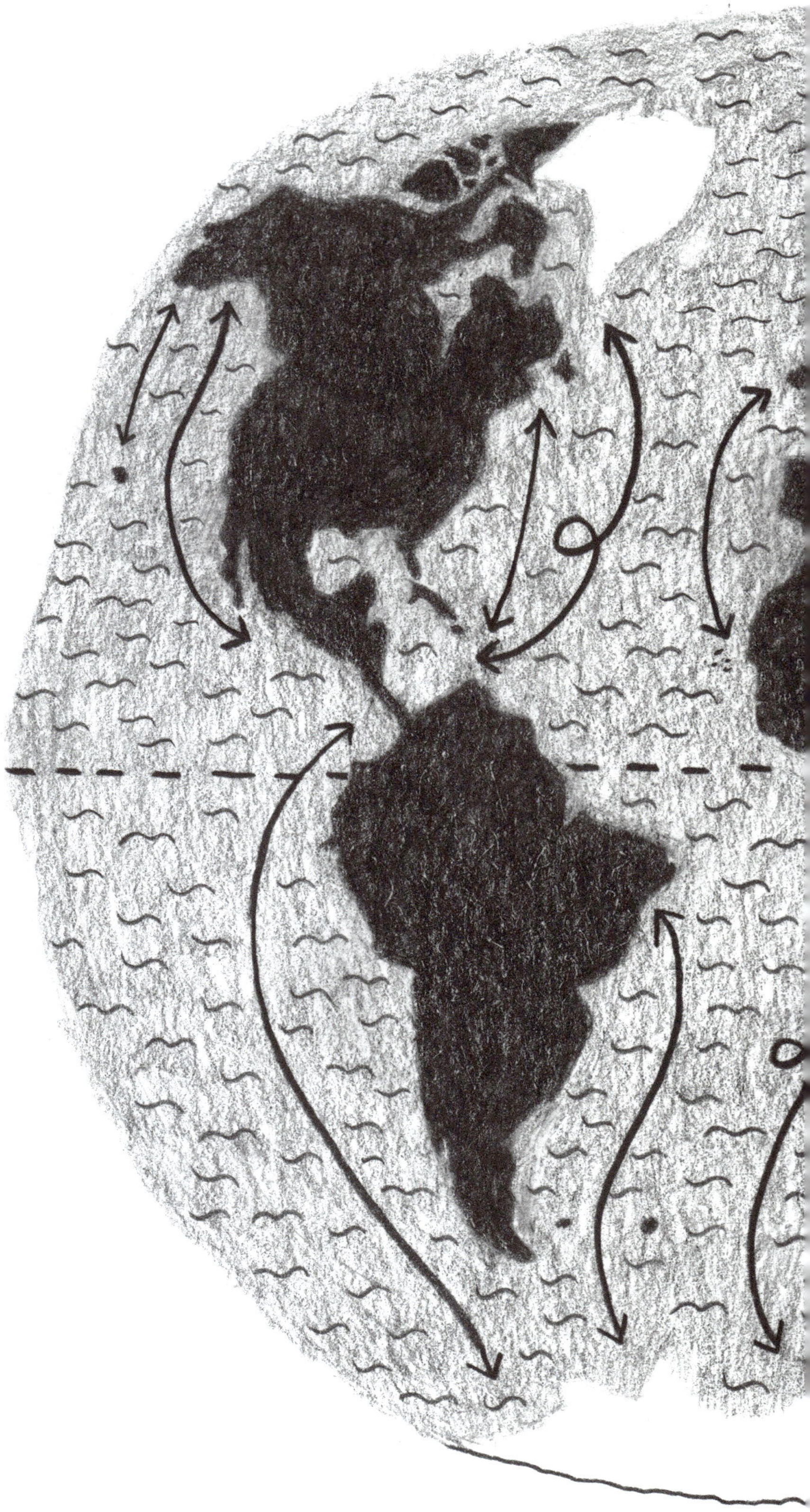

They **reproduce** and start families in the cold season. It is important that newborns start their development in warmer waters: "Let's go! Swim towards the **Equator**".

In the warmer seasons, whales travel towards the poles to **feed** as the ice melts and there are greater numbers of krill and other zooplankton, which are their favourite things to eat.

Among cetaceans, baleen whales are the biggest travellers. Among toothed whales instead, the sperm whale stands out, it travels extensively throughout the year.
Each whale has its own favourite destination. For example, grey whales are famous for their voyages to lagoons on the Mexican coast each winter, before heading north in February to the cold waters around Alaska.
Here you can see some favourite routes of the humpback whale.

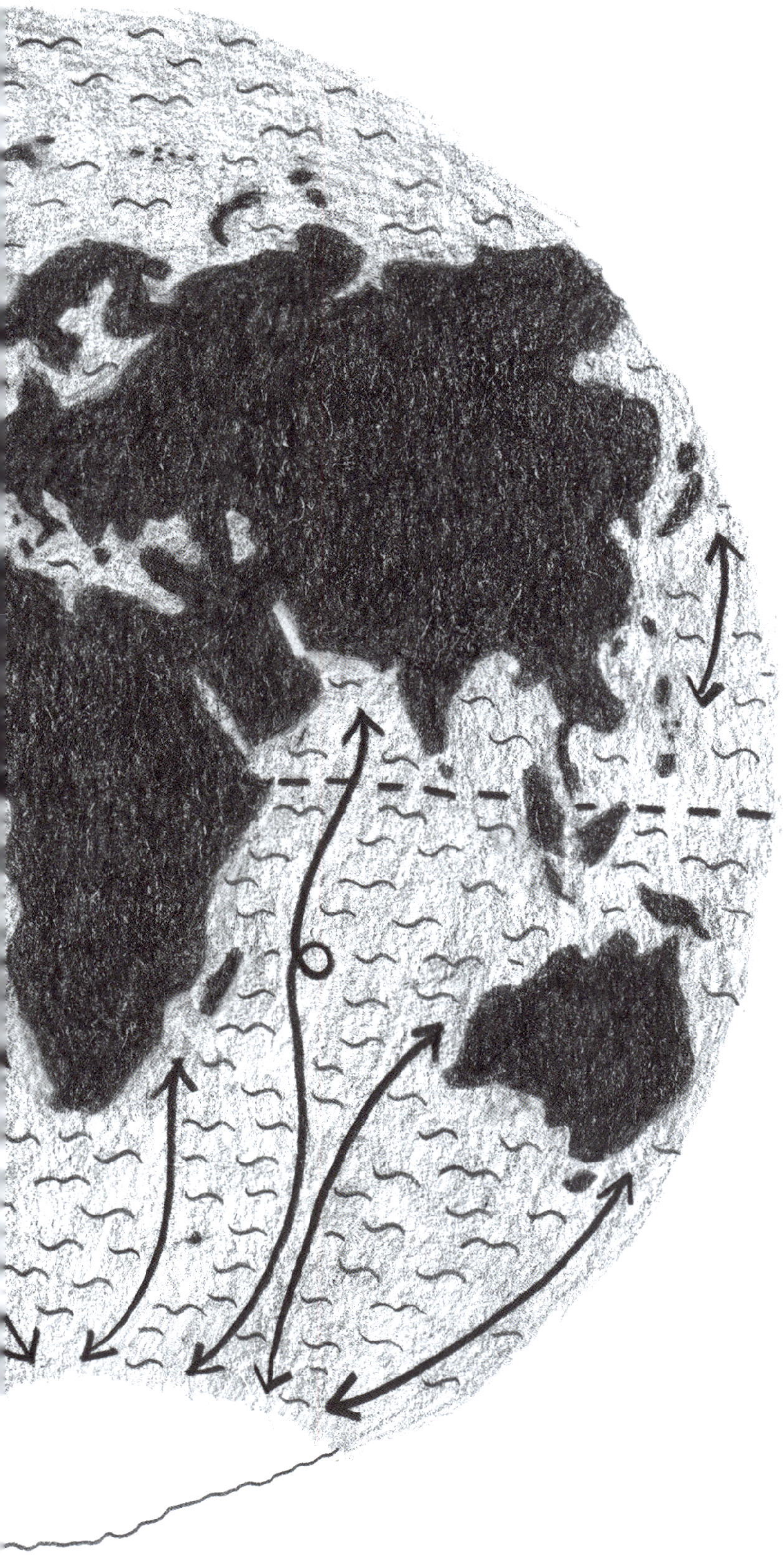

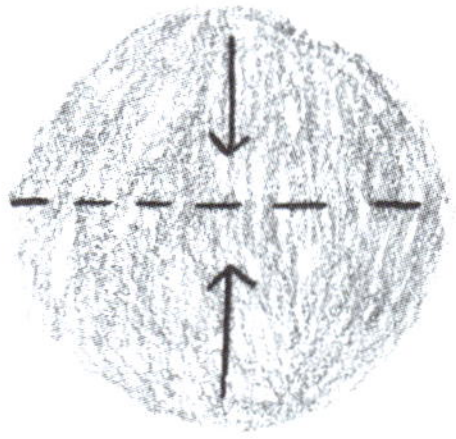

Migration to the **breeding** grounds (winter)

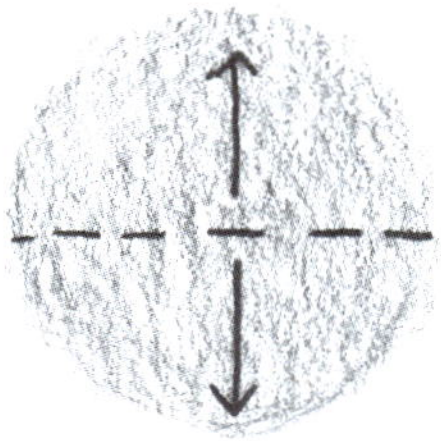

Migration to the **feeding** grounds (summer)

Alone or in good company

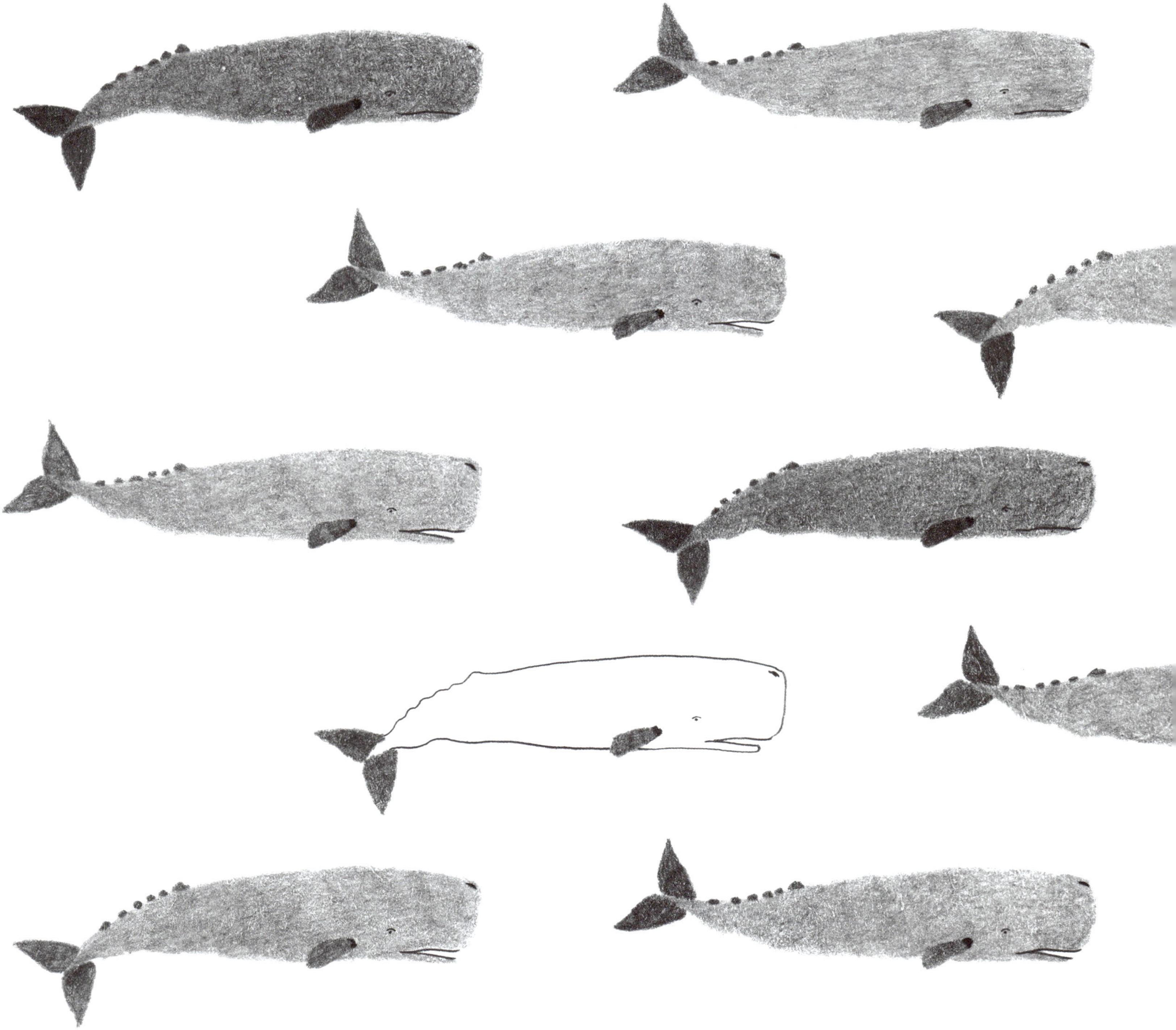

There are no limits to the number of whales that can live in a **pod**.
In some species of cetacean, whales can live alone without any company or others travel in a group consisting of more than one hundred friends.
There is a real social and hierarchical organization in these pods, they work together to get food and protect each other.

A special thing happens with humpback whales: when a baby is born, the mother will be accompanied by an **escort** who will help to protect the calf for a year.
Sperm whales definitely have the biggest pods. There can be as many as 150 members.
Here's one! Look below, there's a pod of sperm whales. If you look closely, you can see a white one, like the famous Moby Dick.

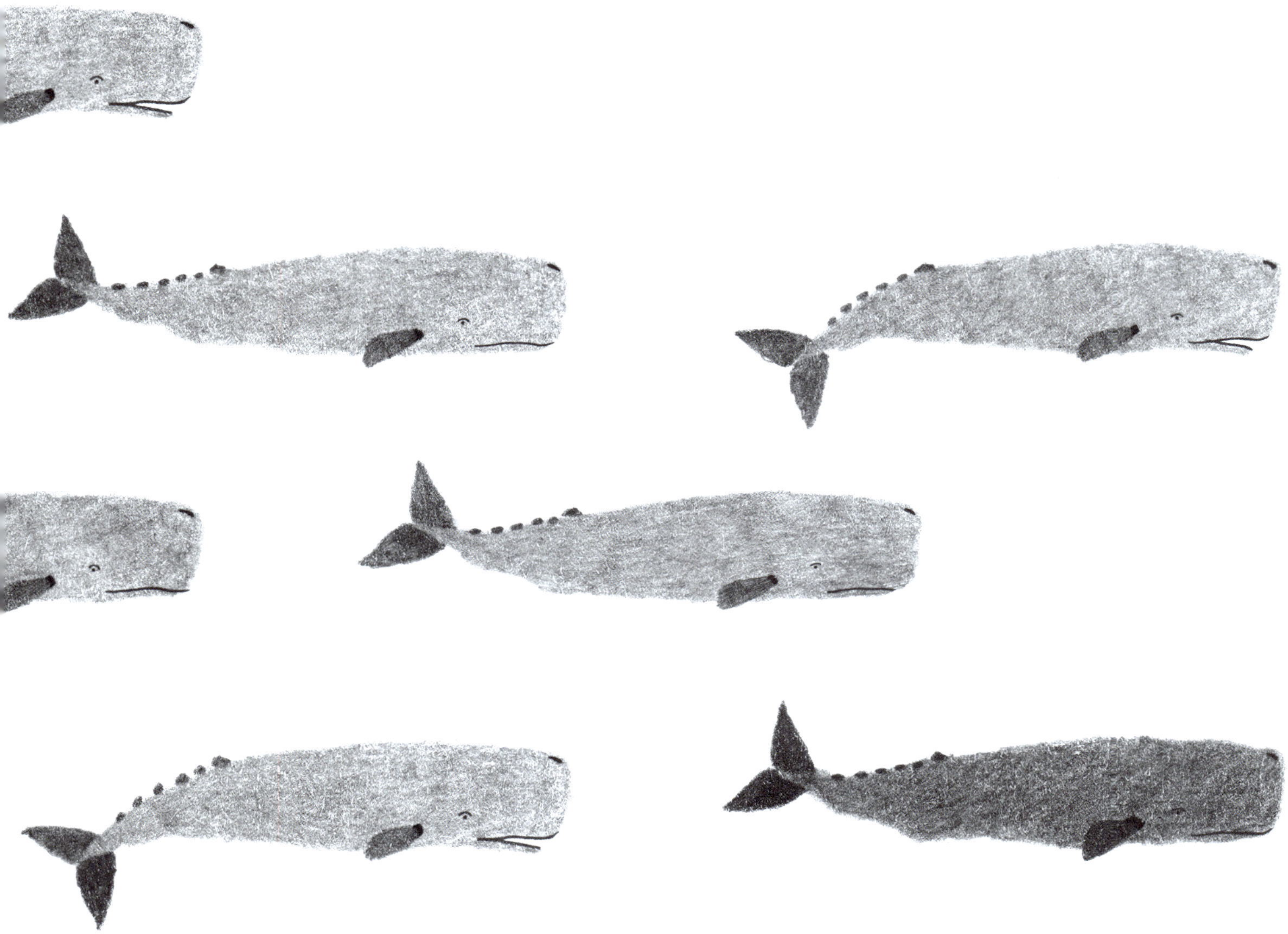

Giants since childhood

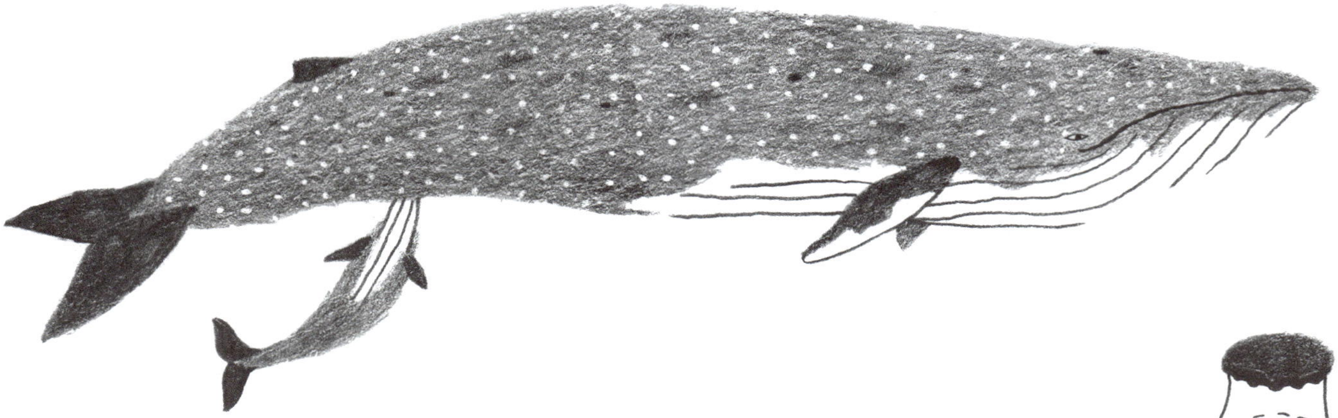

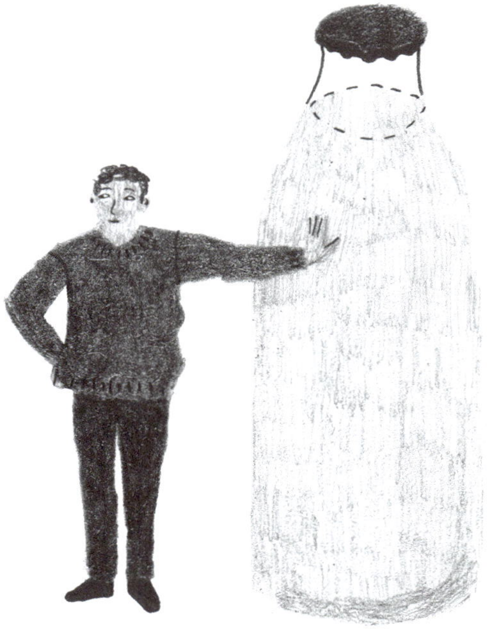

How does a whale's life begin?
Let's start from the beginning.
Pregnancy lasts about a year for all whales, except for sperm whales, who have a gestation period of 18 months. The newborn is already a giant. The pygmy right whale calf, the smallest whale, is already as long as an adult human. And this is nothing compared to a blue whale calf, which is already 7 metres long at birth!
The first thing a newborn must do is breathe so, with the help of their mother, they must get to the surface immediately.
The link between mother and calf is especially close: in the best of cases, they remain together for life!

Milk, milk and more milk
Some whale calves drink up to 400 litres of milk per day. That's a bathtub full!
Nursing lasts for about a year, but some sperm whales, in spite of being grownups, continue to drink unashamedly their mother's milk for around 15 years!

Special partnerships

Barnacles

Whales are so big that some animals confuse them for a place to live.
This is precisely what happens with **barnacles**. Contrary to what many think, **they are not parasites like whale lice**, who feed by sucking blood.
Barnacles are only **guests** on the bodies of large cetaceans; they live on them but don’t feed from them. These small animals are crustaceans.
They live inside pointed shells, so that they are also called *dogteeth*.

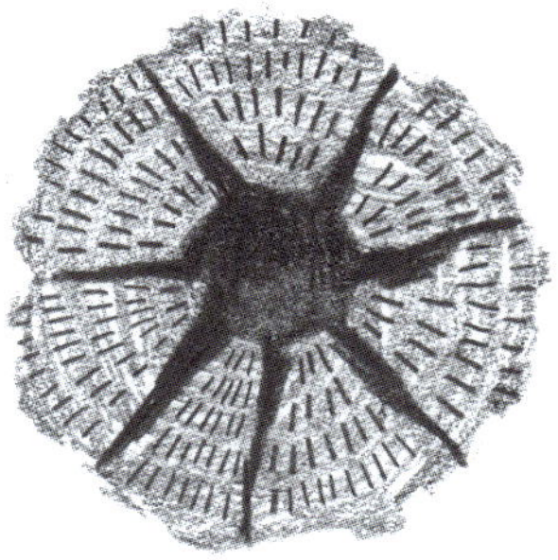

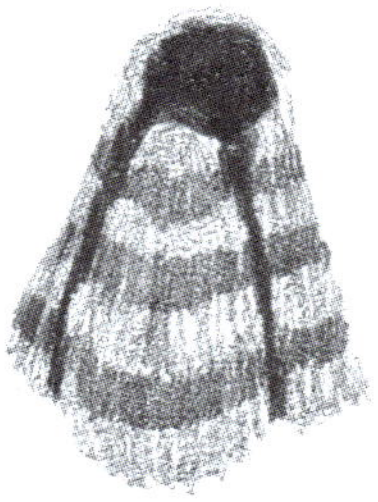

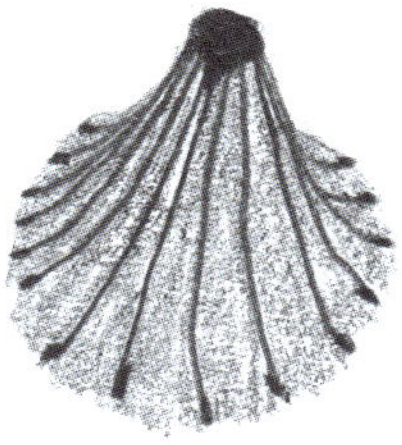

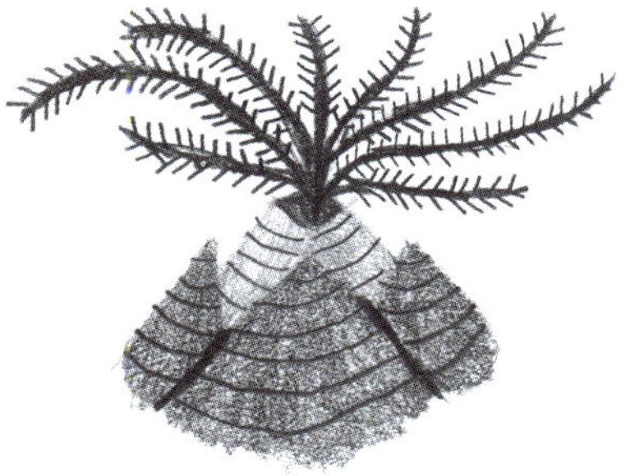

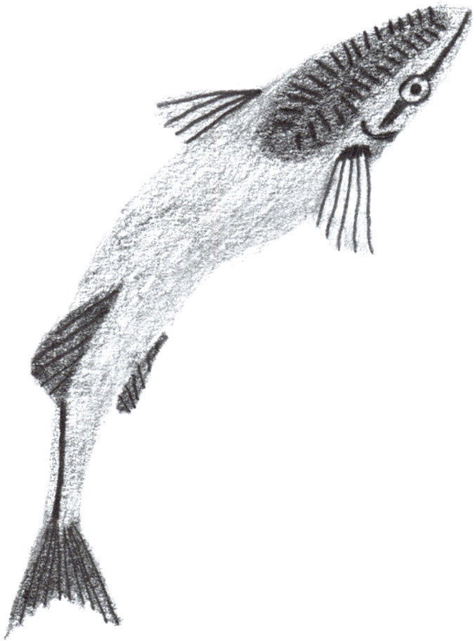

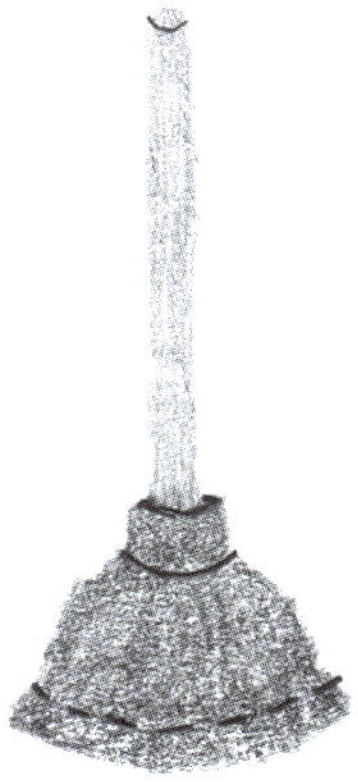

Remoras

Whereas barnacles see whales as somewhere to live, **remoras** instead think of them as a type of public transport.
These fish have a special talent, a part of their head can attach to surface like a **sucker.**
Remoras attach themselves to whales in order to travel quicker and, indirectly, receive protection from predators, who are awed by their big travel companions.

And humans?

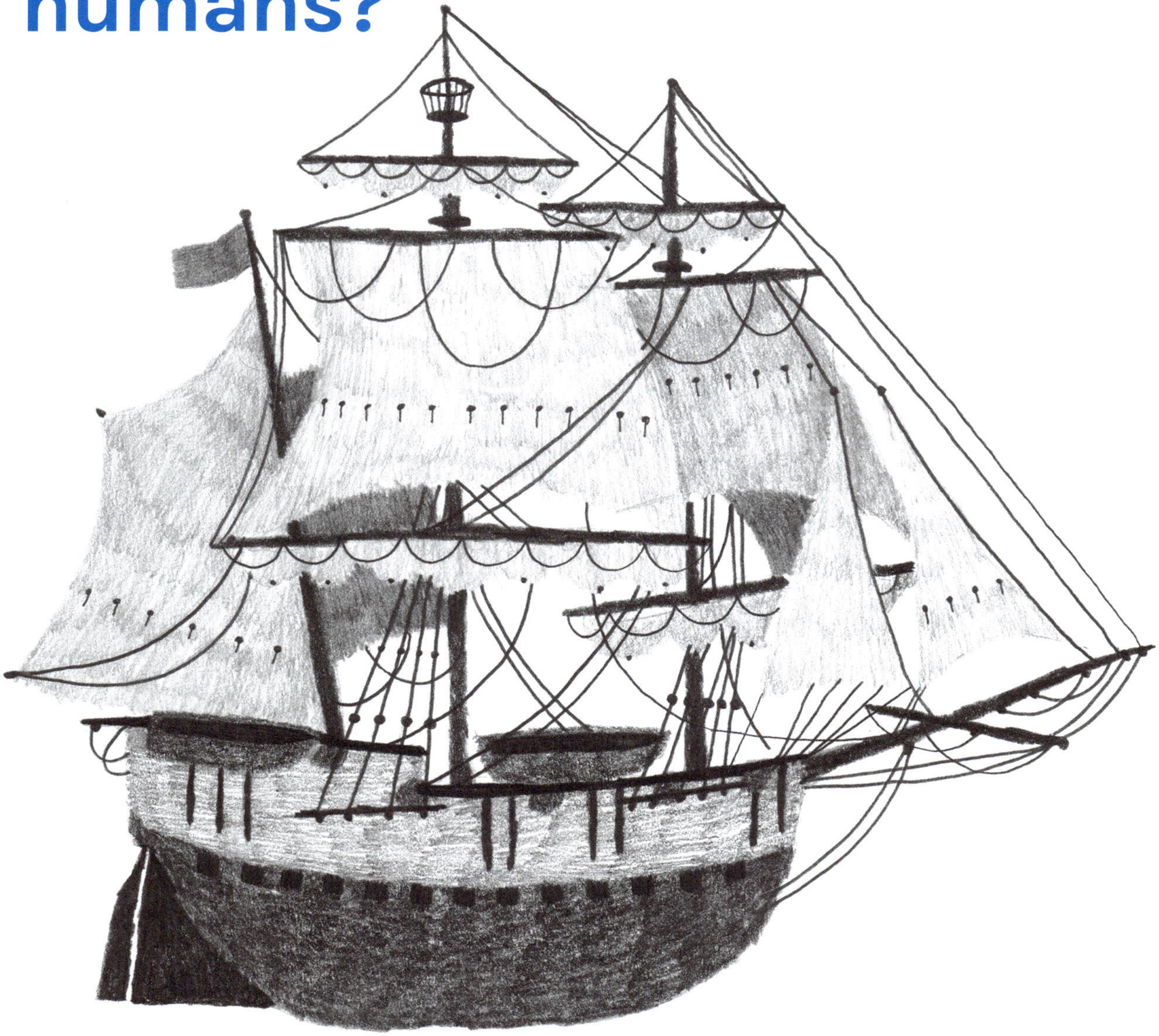

Hunting

Unfortunately, the relationship between whales and humans is mainly defined by **hunting**. Hunting has ancient origins. Norwegian people were already hunting in 2000 B.C., but its most popular period was between 1700 and 1800. Whale meat is not that tasty, humans hunted them more for the **oil** that was extracted from the fat, which was even known as "liquid gold."

It had a number of different uses, but it was mainly used to light lanterns at home.
In 1986, after the critical decline of marine mammal populations, whale hunting was fortunately outlawed worldwide.
Unfortunately, there are still those who try to get around those rules, even nowadays.

Captain Ahab is the most famous whale hunter in literature. His greatest obsession was Moby Dick, the white sperm whale that he never stopped chasing.

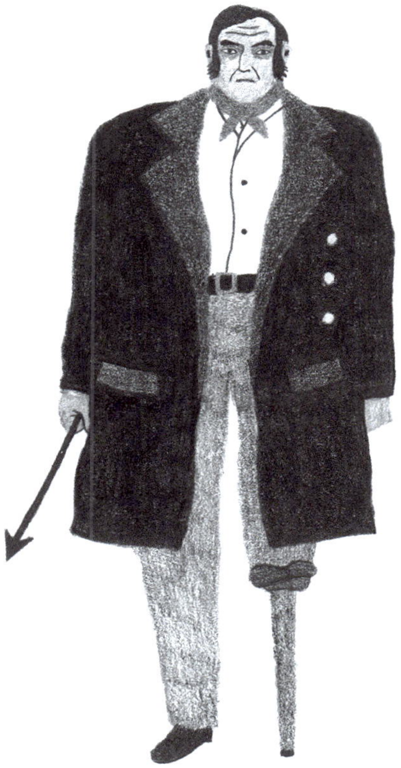

There are indigenous populations who continue to practice whaling using **traditional methods**. As they live in some of the coldest parts of the world, whale hunting is necessary for their survival.

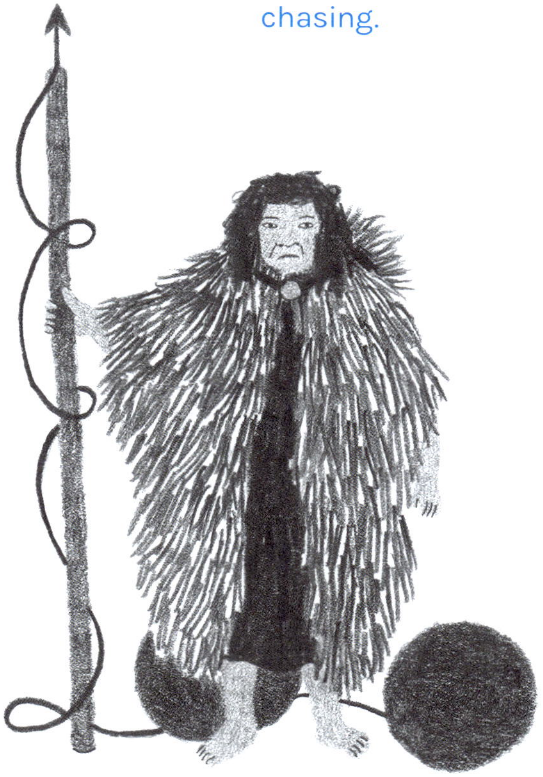

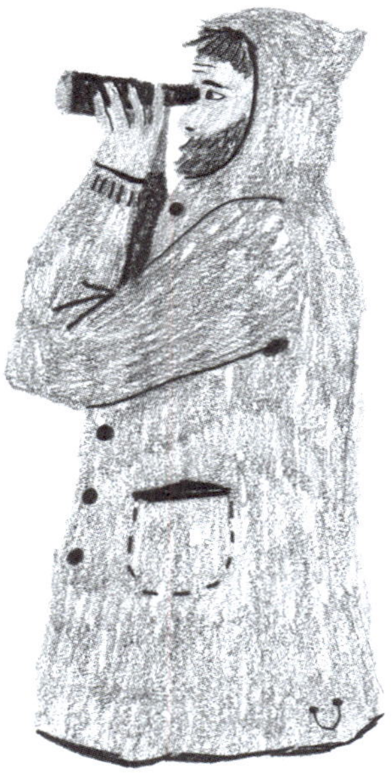

Whale watching

Not everyone has bad intentions, however. **Whale watching** means taking a trip to the middle of the sea, trying to meet these giant mammals and maybe even getting a photograph of them. You can go whale watching in many parts of the world. In Italy, whale watching trips are mainly held in Liguria.

One by one

Right whale

Eubalaena australis
Eubalaena glacialis
Order: Cetacea
Suborder: Mysticeti
Family: Whale

Length: 11-18 metres
Weight: 30-80 tonnes

The right whale's skin is completely black.

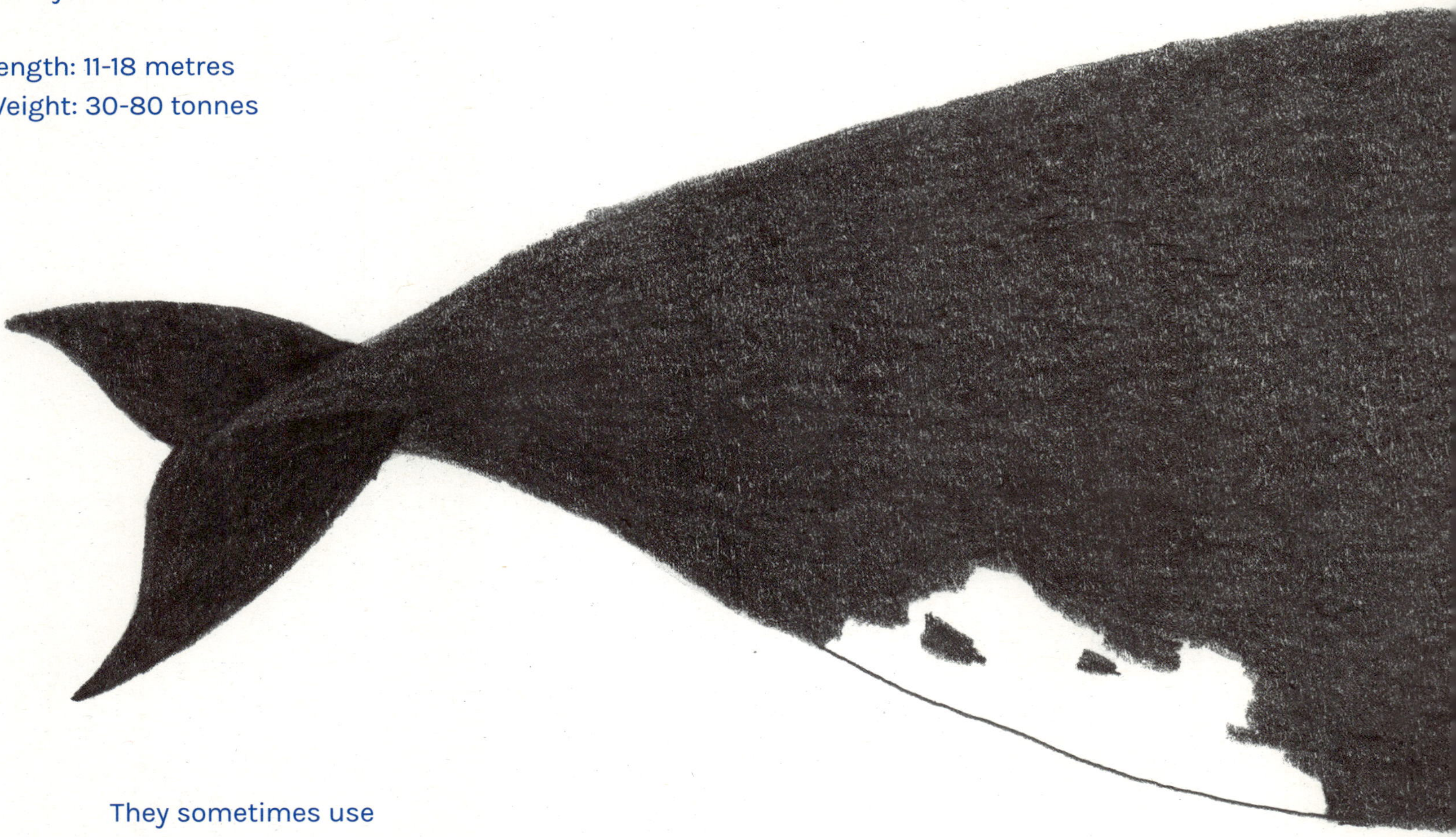

They sometimes use their **tail fin** like a ship's sail to play.

The only white spot is visible on the belly.

The **blow** has a typical V shape
and it can reach up to 5 metres.

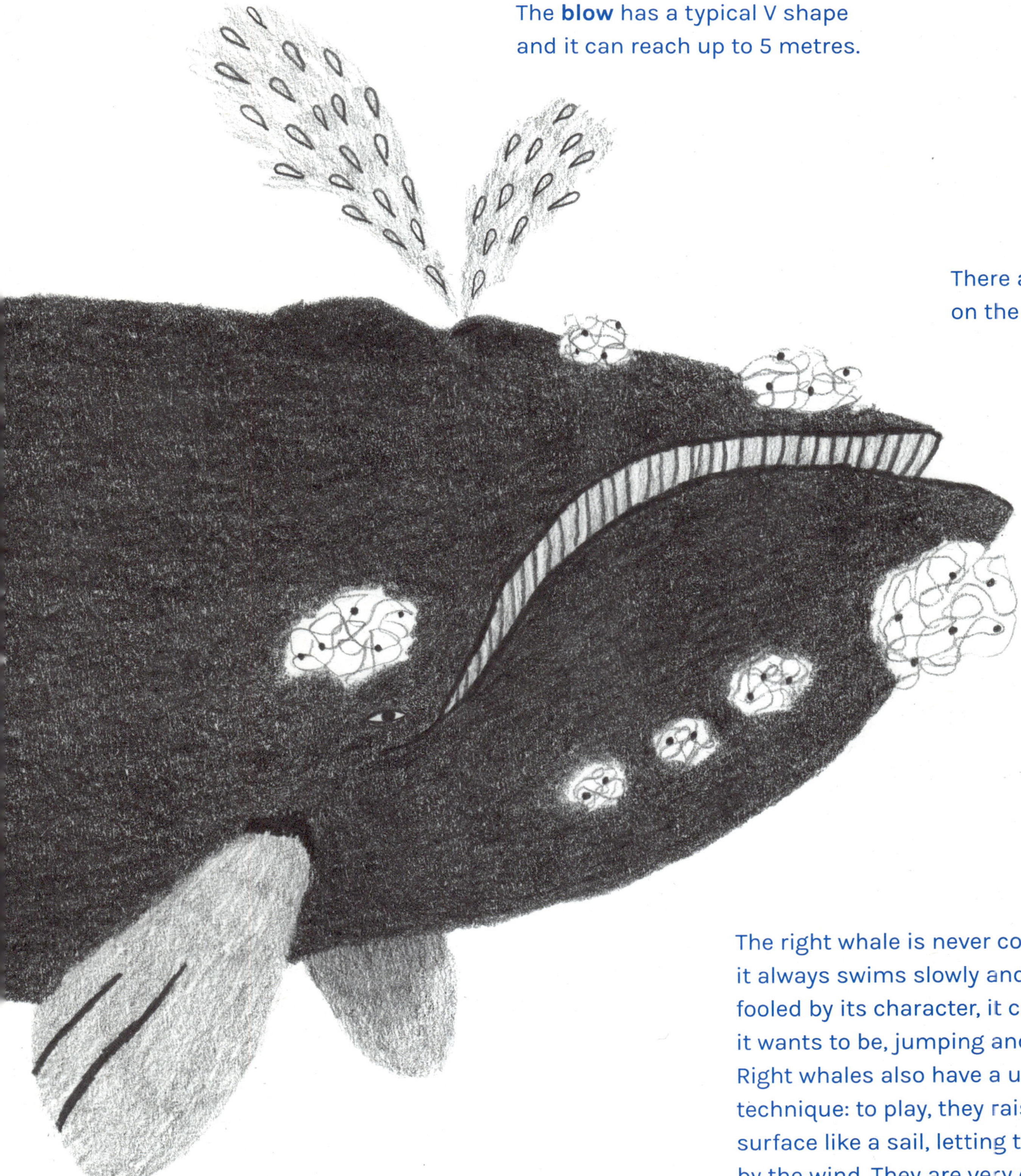

There are usually many **callous**
on the top of the nose and chin.

The right whale is never concerned with speed, it always swims slowly and quietly. Don't be fooled by its character, it can be athletic when it wants to be, jumping and performing stunts. Right whales also have a unique swimming technique: to play, they raise their tail to the surface like a sail, letting themselves be carried by the wind. They are very cautious whales, they only emerge to the surface one at a time when in a group.

Bowhead whale

Balaena mysticetus
Order: Cetacea
Suborder: Mysticeti
Family: Whales

Length: 14-18 metres
Weight: 60-100 tonnes

Its colour varies from black to bluish.

Some bowheads have a light spot near the **tail fin**.

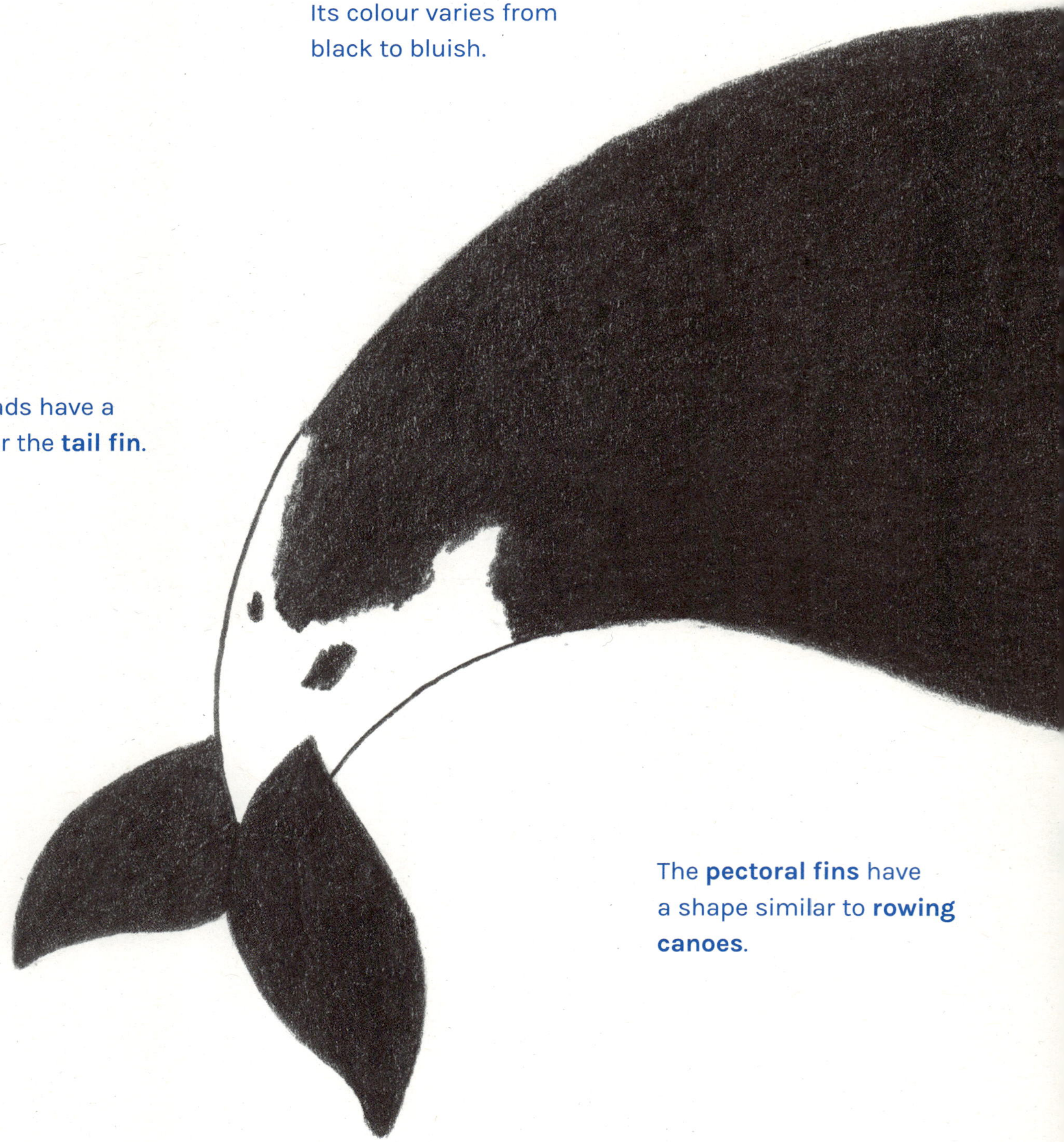

The **pectoral fins** have a shape similar to **rowing canoes**.

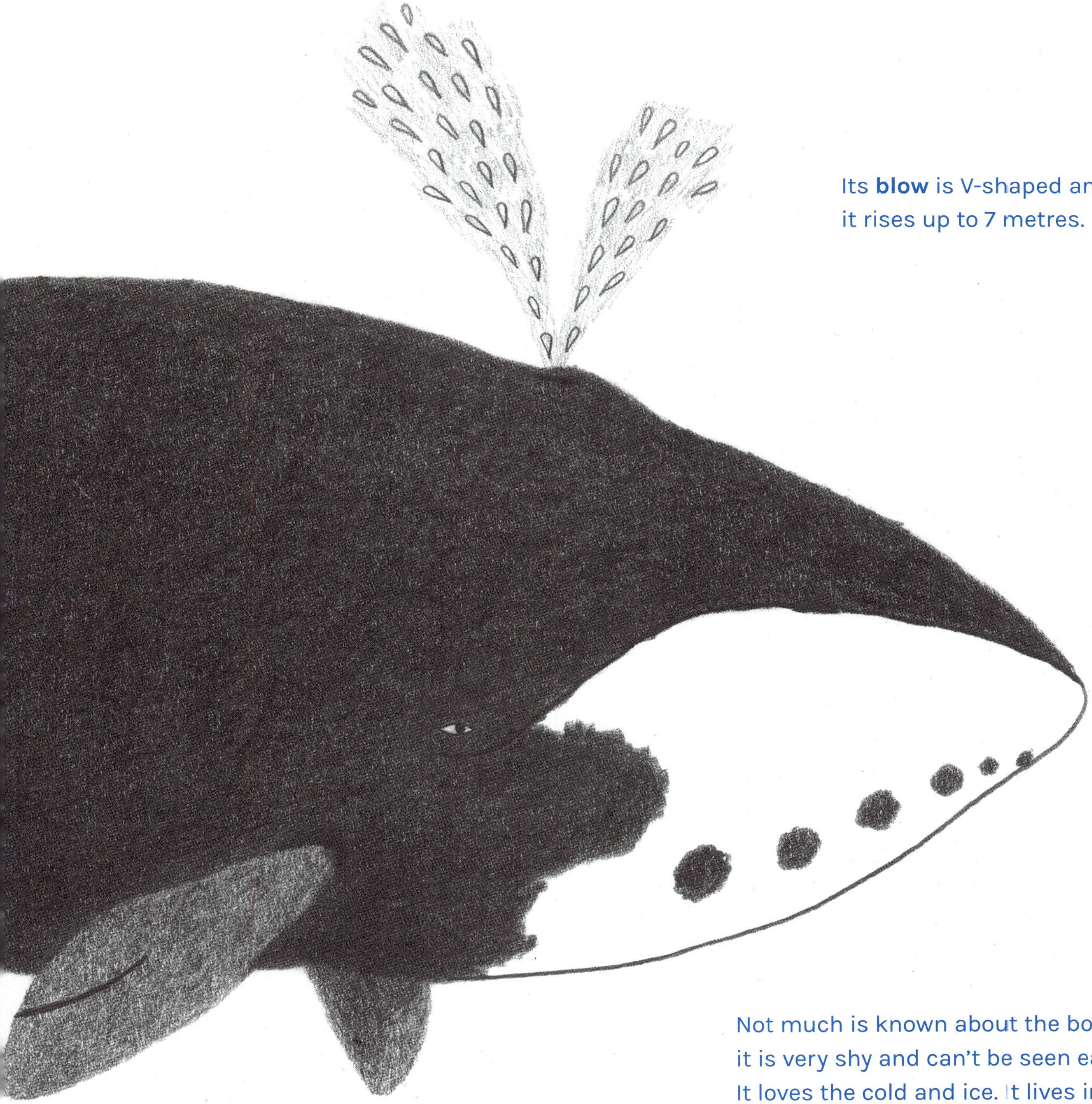

Its **blow** is V-shaped and
it rises up to 7 metres.

Not much is known about the bowhead whale, it is very shy and can't be seen easily.
It loves the cold and ice. It lives in the waters surrounding the North Pole, chasing the layers of floating ice that retreats and expands with the changing temperature.
In order to breathe, it sometimes has to pierce the layer of ice to get its head through.

Its most characteristic feature is a large white patch under the chin.

Pygmy right whale

Caperea marginata
Order: Cetacea
Suborder: Mysticeti
Family: Neobalaenidae

Length: 5.5-6.5 metres
Weight: 3-3.5 tonnes

It has a **dorsal fin**, despite not being a rorqual.

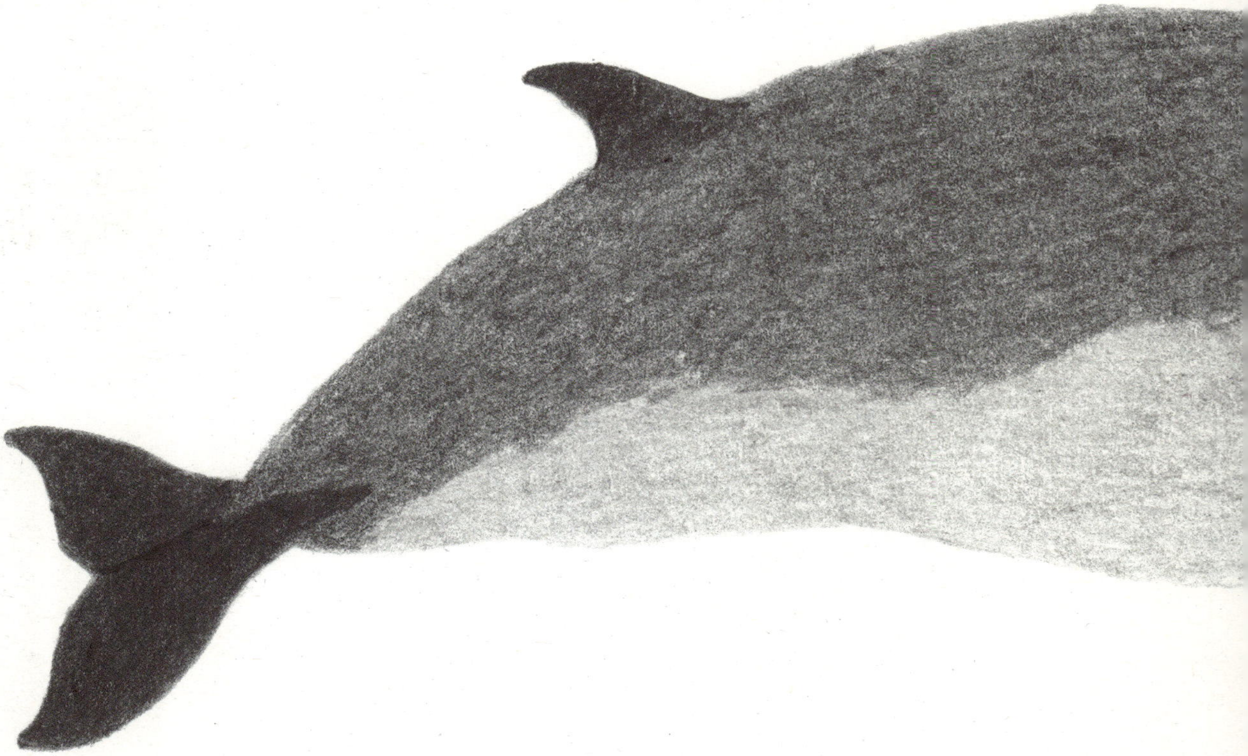

Its belly is lighter in colour than its back, which can vary from light grey to white.

It is difficult to recognise the pygmy right whale from its **blow**, as it is often small and indistinct.

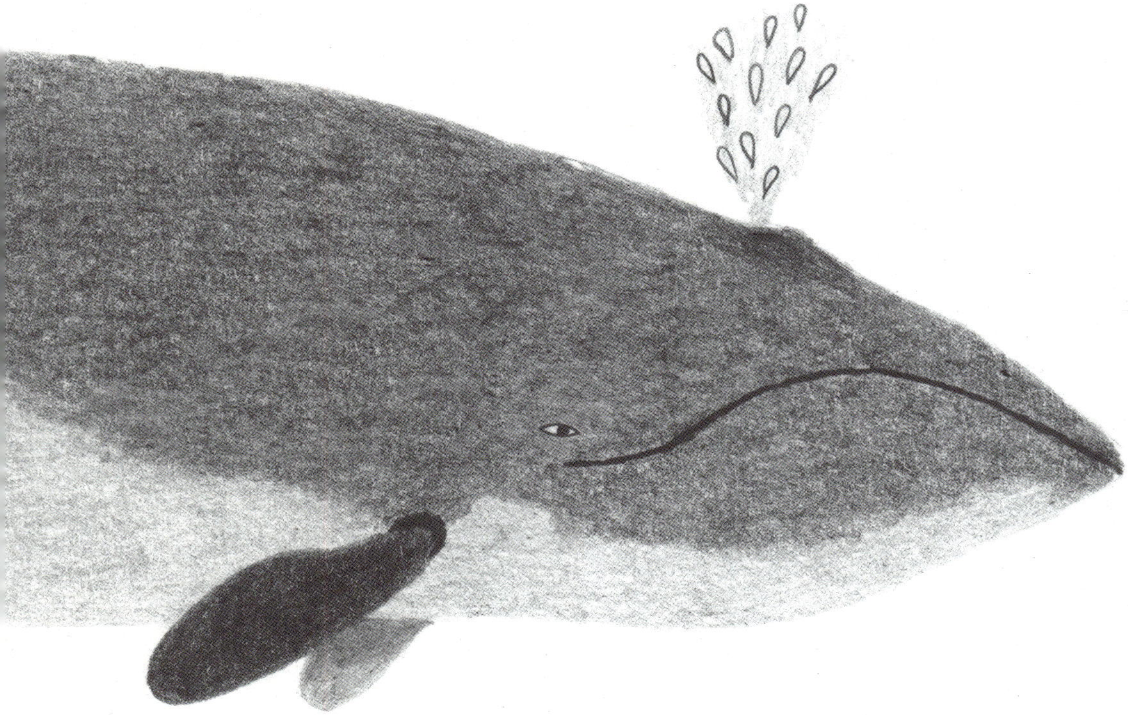

Its **pectoral fins** are dark on one side and light on the other.

The pygmy right whale is the smallest of all whales. When we say small, it is still taller than four people! They are said to be rare, but they are probably just shy and hide from prying eyes. They are only shy with humans though, because you can sometimes see them swimming with other types of whales.

Grey whale

Eschrichtius robustus
Order: Cetacea
Suborder: Mysticeti
Family: Eschrichtiidae

Length: 12-14 metres
Weight: 15-35 tonnes

It has a hump on its back, which seems to be a hint to the **dorsal fin**.

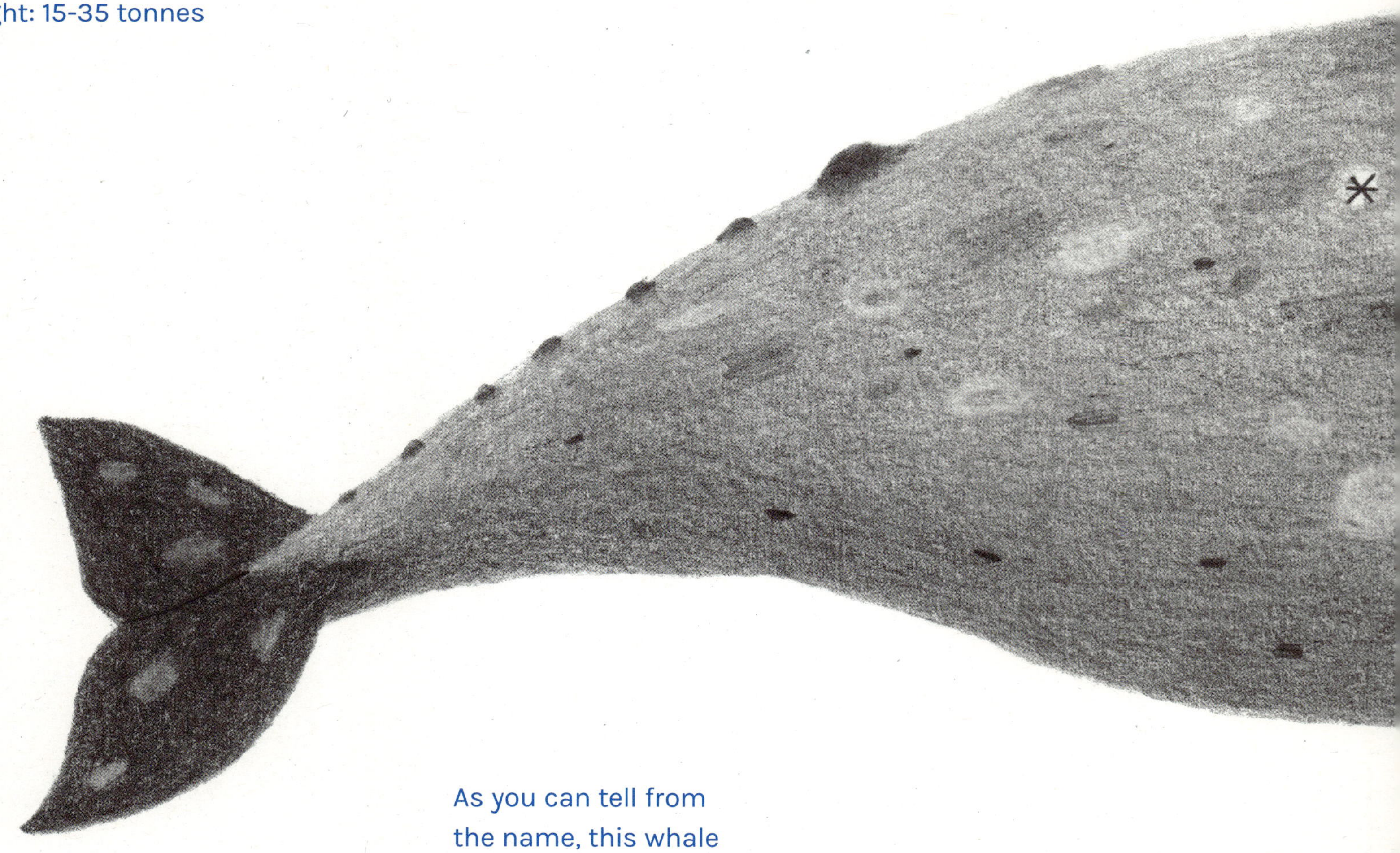

As you can tell from the name, this whale is famous for its grey colour.

Its V-shaped **blow**
can reach up to 4 metres
in height.

Its body can get infested
with **whale lice** and **barnacles**.

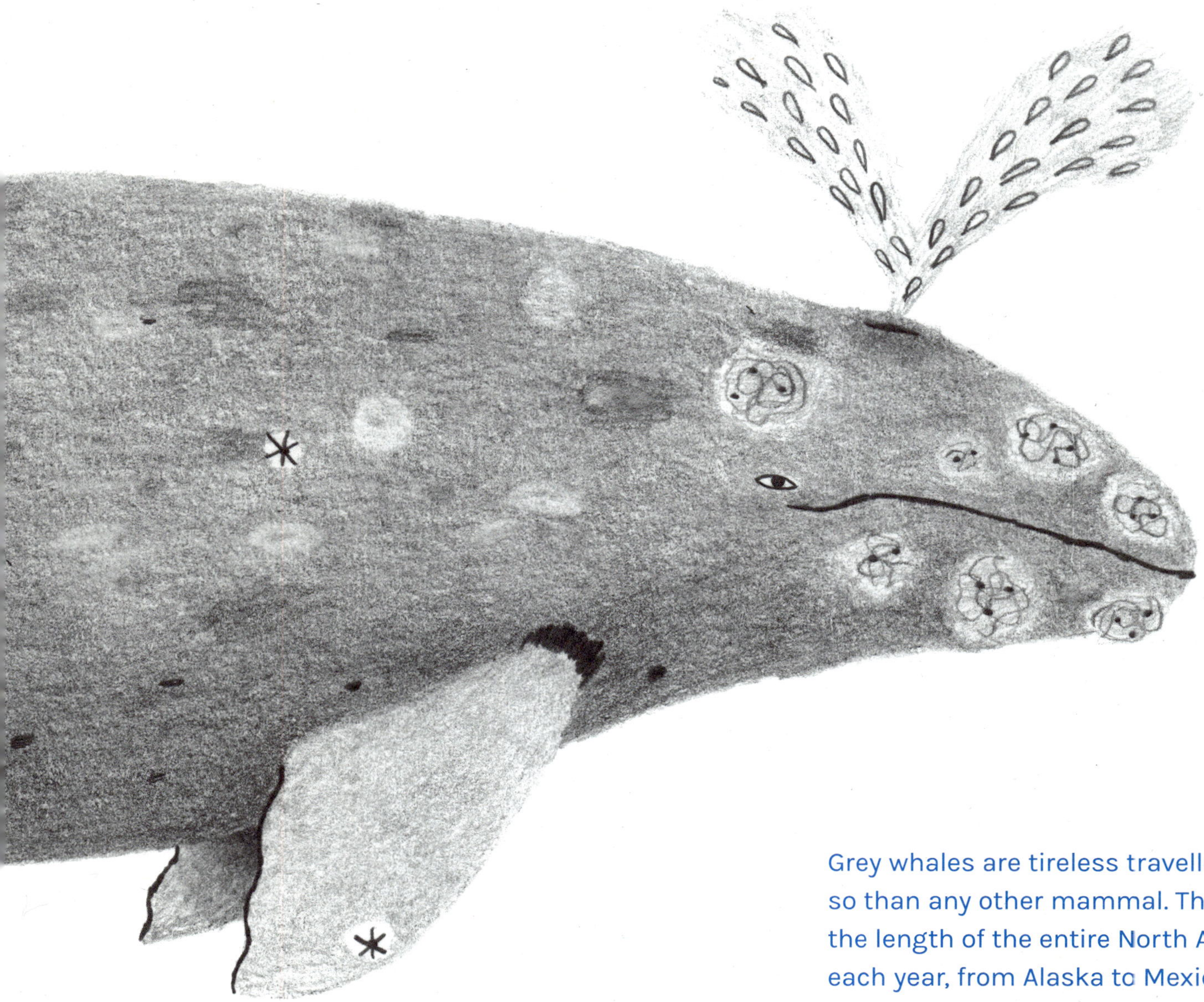

Grey whales are tireless travellers, more so than any other mammal. They travel the length of the entire North American coast each year, from Alaska to Mexico. The whole roundtrip, that's more than 20,000 km! They are the only whales that feed on the seabed, filtering the sand in search of small crustaceans. They are also friendly towards humans, letting us touch and stroke them without too much fear.

Humpback whale

Megaptera novaeangliae
Order: Cetacea
Suborder: Mysticeti
Family: Rorqual

Length: 11.5-15 metres
Weight: 25-30 tonnes

It has dark coloured skin, passing from blue and black to dark grey.

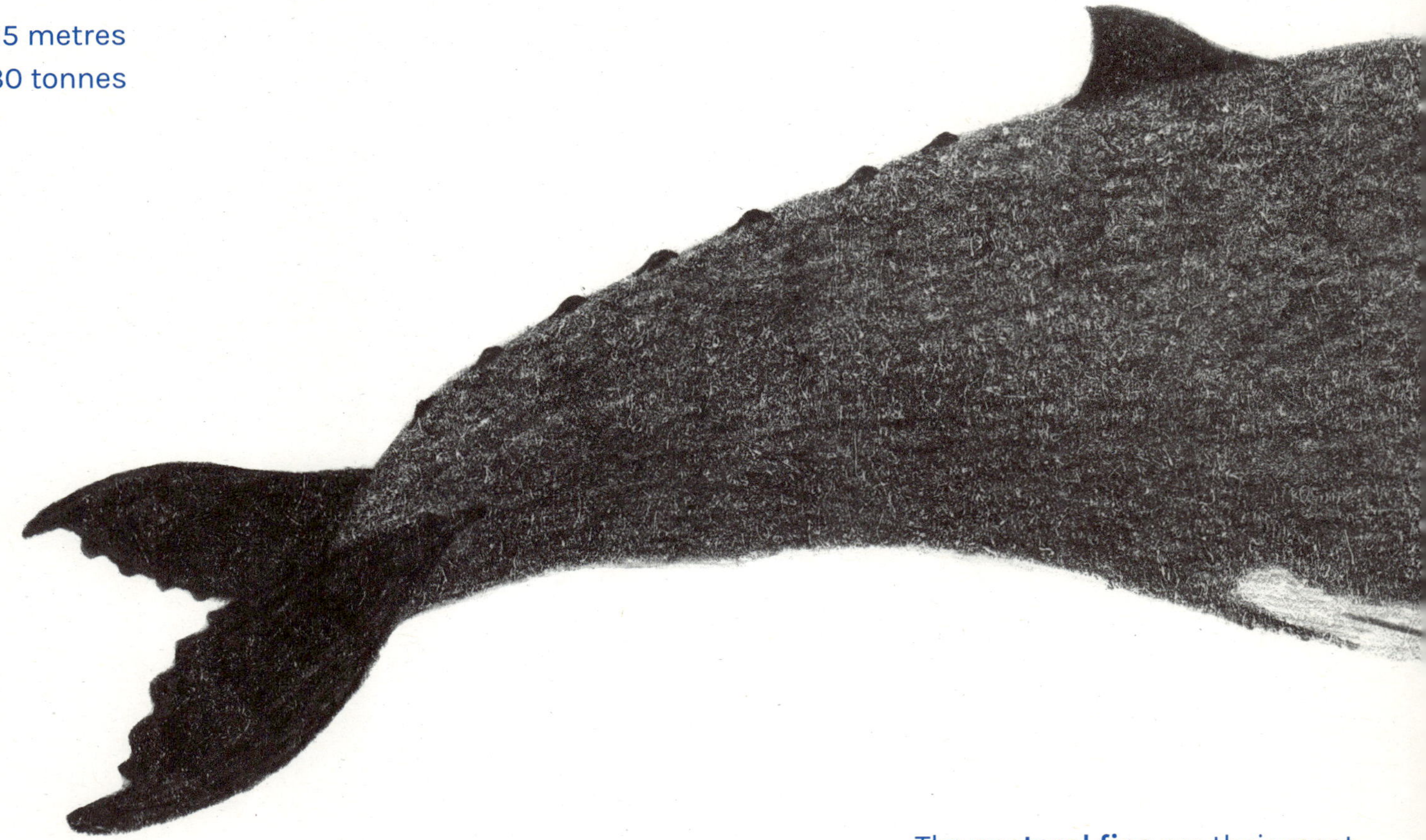

The white pigment under the **tail** is different for each whale, like our fingertips.

The **pectoral fins** are their most characteristic feature: they are very long, and can reach up to 5 metres. It is no coincidence that in Greek, their name *megaptere* means "large wings."

Its **blow** is wider than
it is tall, reaching up
to 3 metres.

It has a lumpy head.

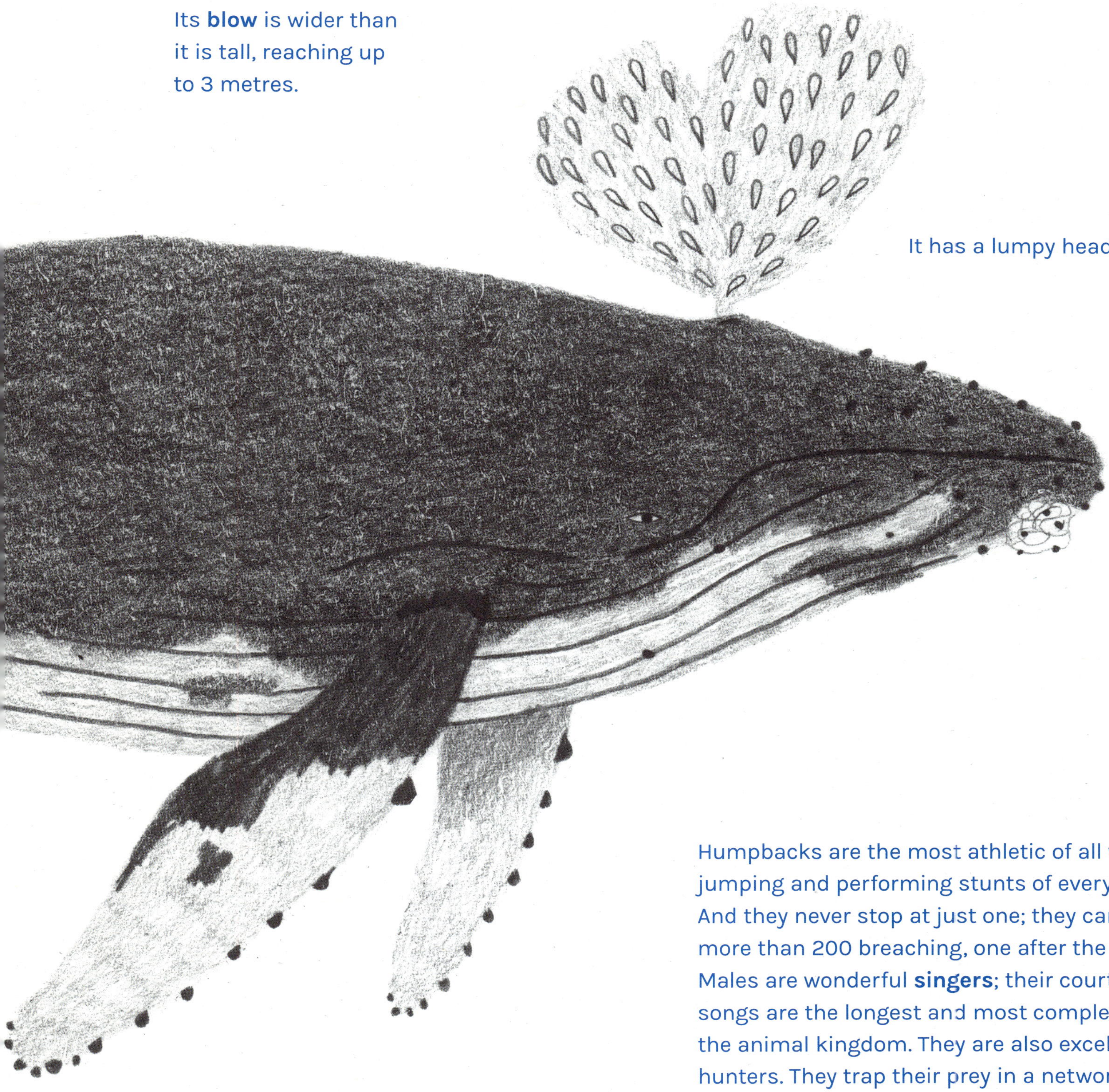

Humpbacks are the most athletic of all whales, jumping and performing stunts of every kind. And they never stop at just one; they can do more than 200 breaching, one after the other! Males are wonderful **singers**; their courtship songs are the longest and most complex in the animal kingdom. They are also excellent hunters. They trap their prey in a network of bubbles, circling around them repeatedly.

Blue whale

Balaenoptera musculus
Order: Cetacea
Suborder: Mysticeti
Family: Rorqual

Length: 24-30 metres
Weight: 120-180 tonnes

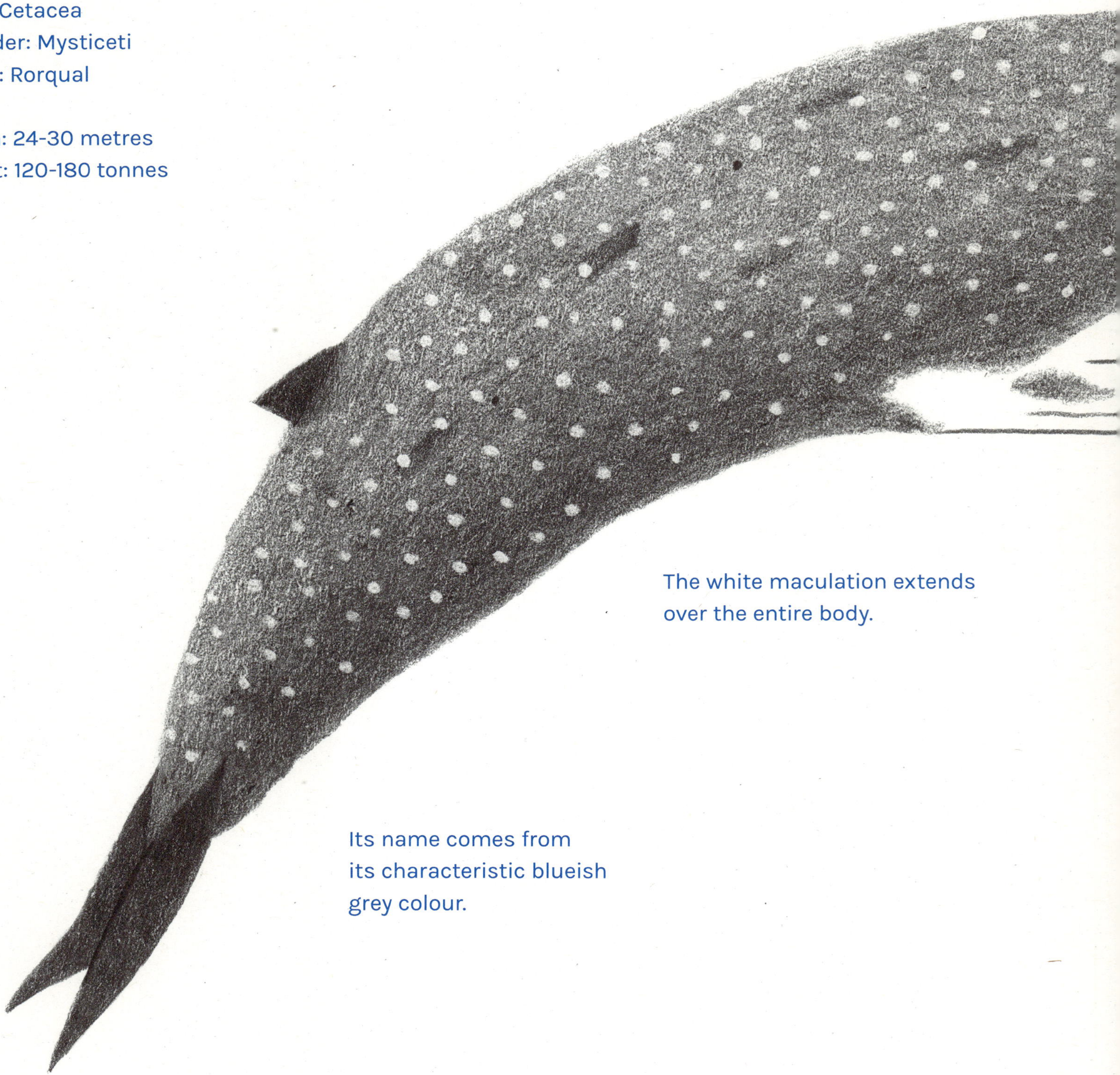

The white maculation extends over the entire body.

Its name comes from its characteristic blueish grey colour.

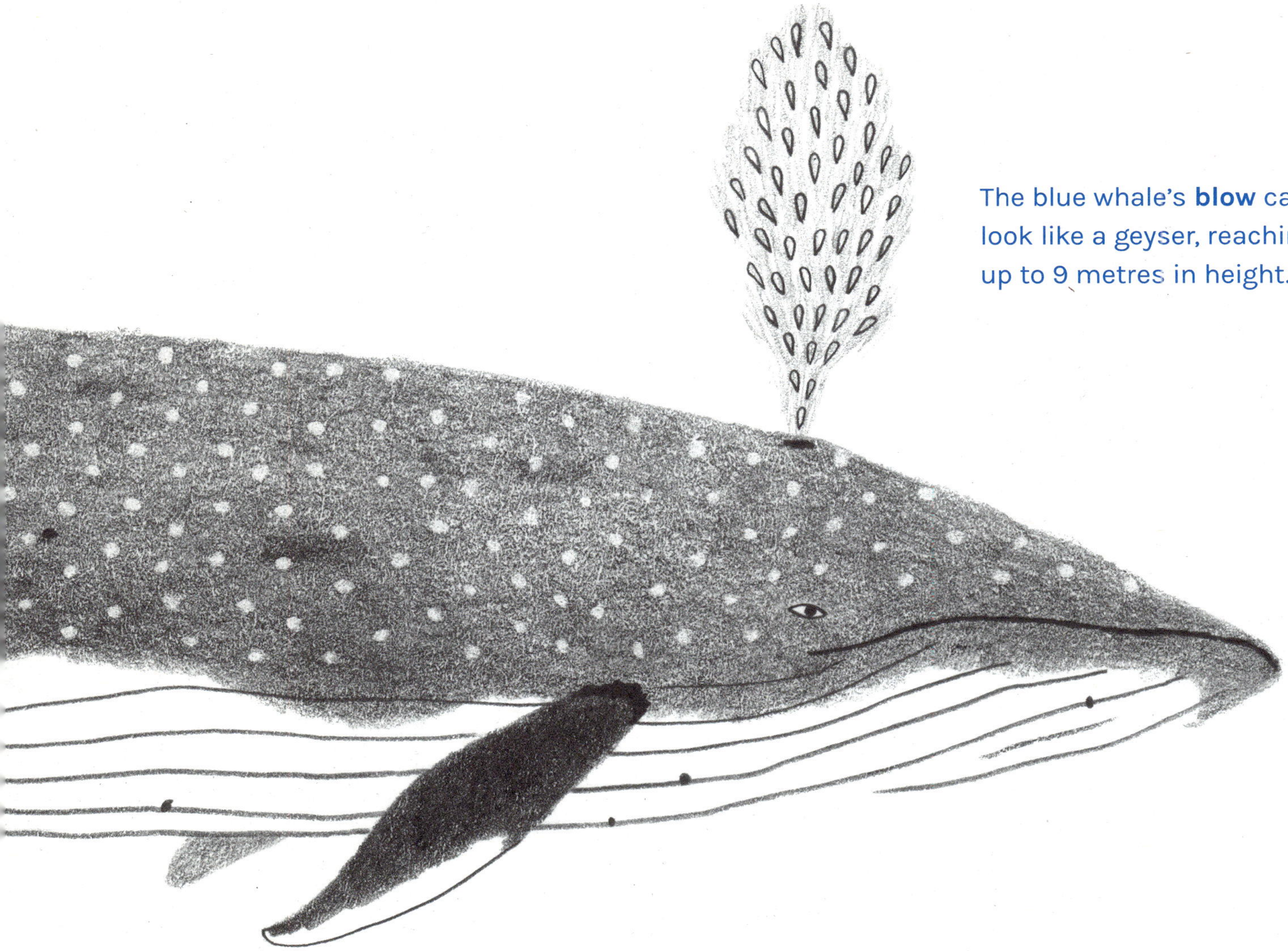

The blue whale's **blow** can look like a geyser, reaching up to 9 metres in height.

It has a light coloured belly, with up to 90 **folds of skin**.

The blue whale is the biggest animal on the planet, surpassing all others, including most extinct animals. To maintain its size, it needs to eat in abundance, devouring up to four tonnes of krill each day! But not everything heavy is slow. Despite its size, the blue whale is very fast, reaching speeds of up to 30 km per hour.

Fin whale

Balaenoptera physalus
Order: Cetacea
Suborder: Mysticeti
Family: Rorqual

Length: 18-22 metres
Weight: 30-80 tonnes

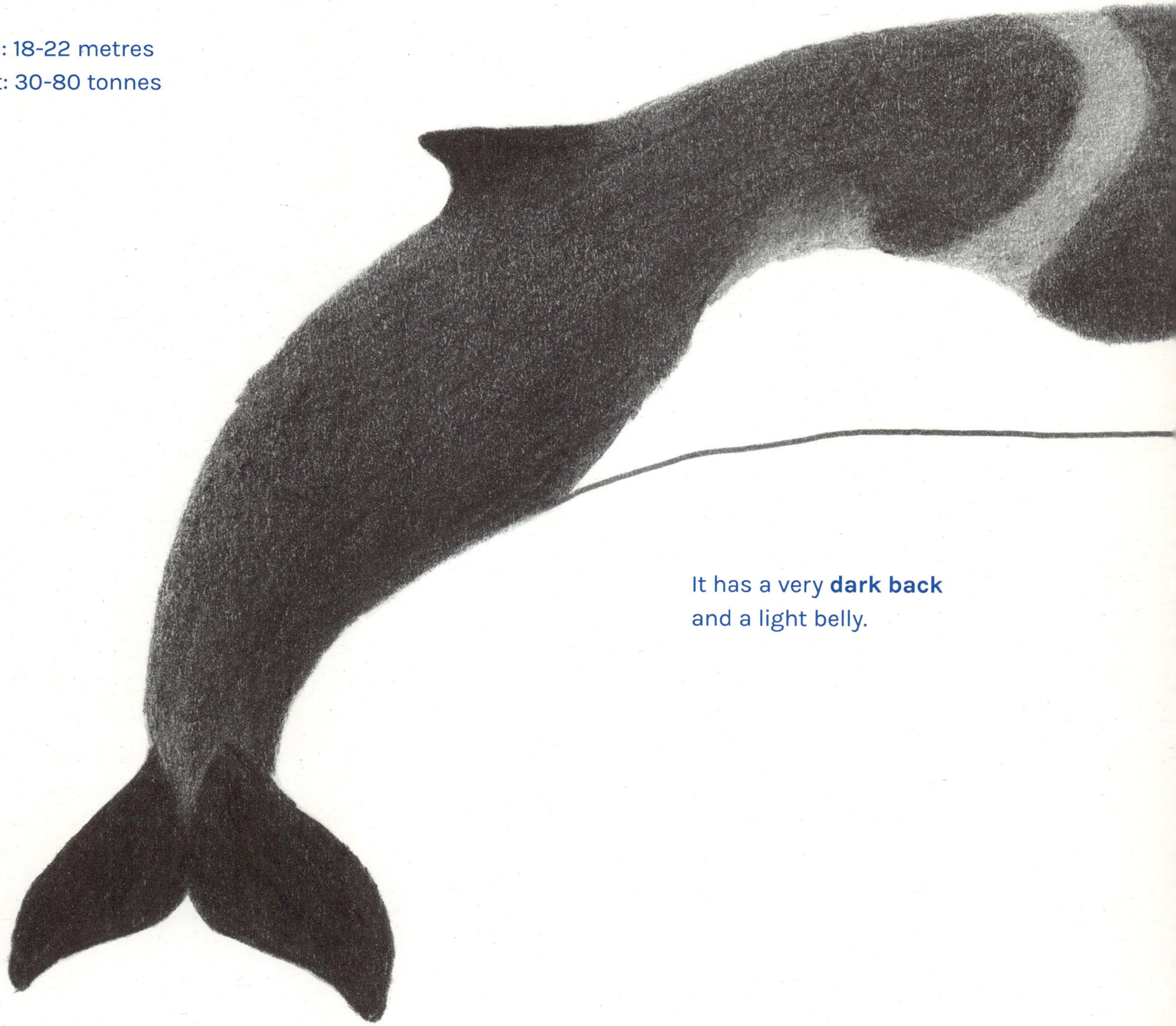

It has a very **dark back** and a light belly.

There are lighter patterns along the **back**.

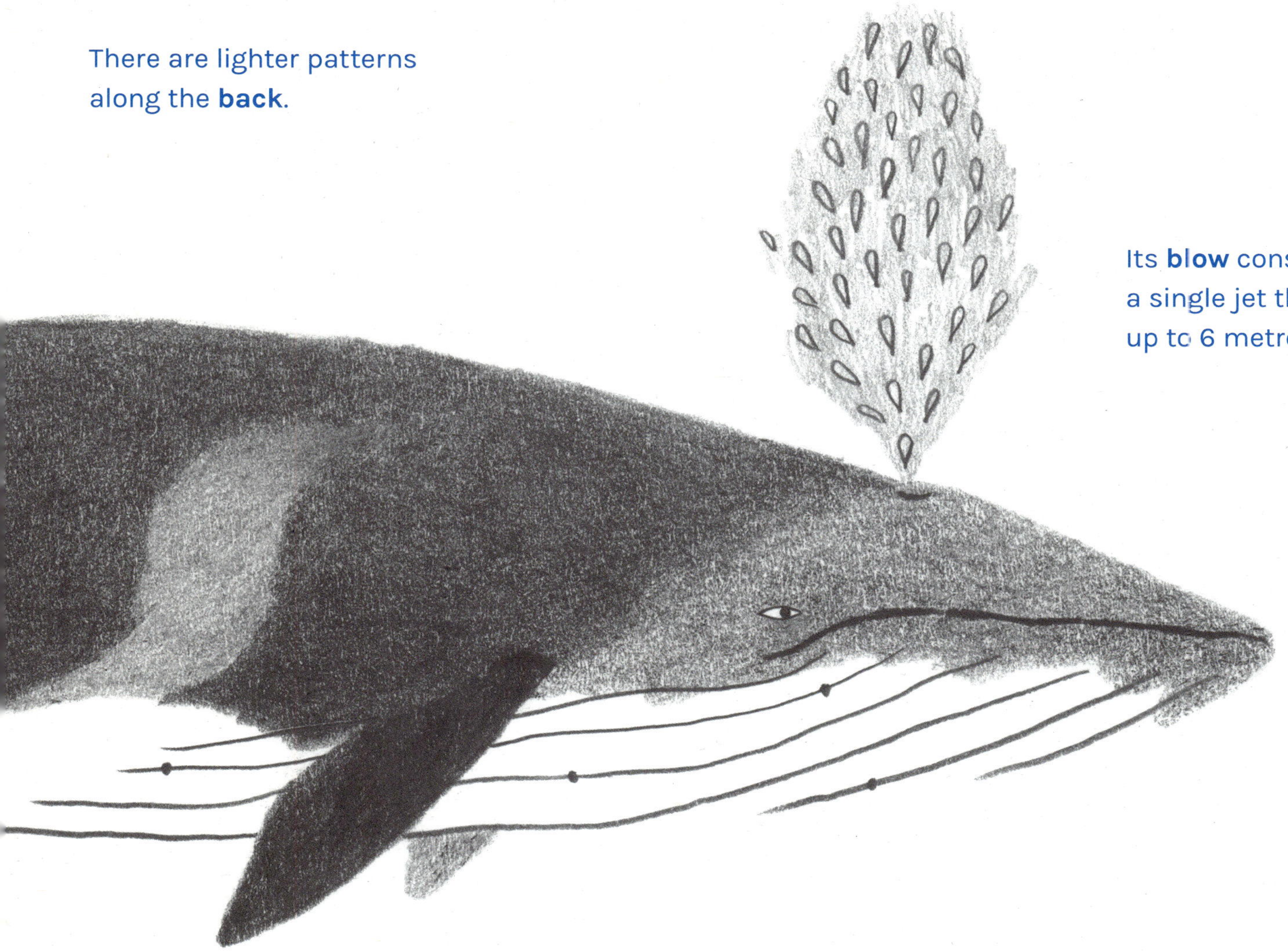

Its **blow** consists of a single jet that reaches up to 6 metres.

The colouring of the chin is **asymmetrical**: the right side is white, while the left side is dark like the back.

The fin whale is the second largest animal in the world, after the blue whale. They look quite similar, and you can easily confuse one for the other especially if seen in passing. It is one of the most common whales in waters north of the equator, and it can even be spotted in the Mediterranean.

Minke whale

Balaenoptera acutorostrata
Order: Cetacea
Suborder: Mysticeti
Family: Rorqual

Length: 7-10 metres
Weight: 5-15 tonnes

Its **dorsal fin** is the most developed of all rorquals.

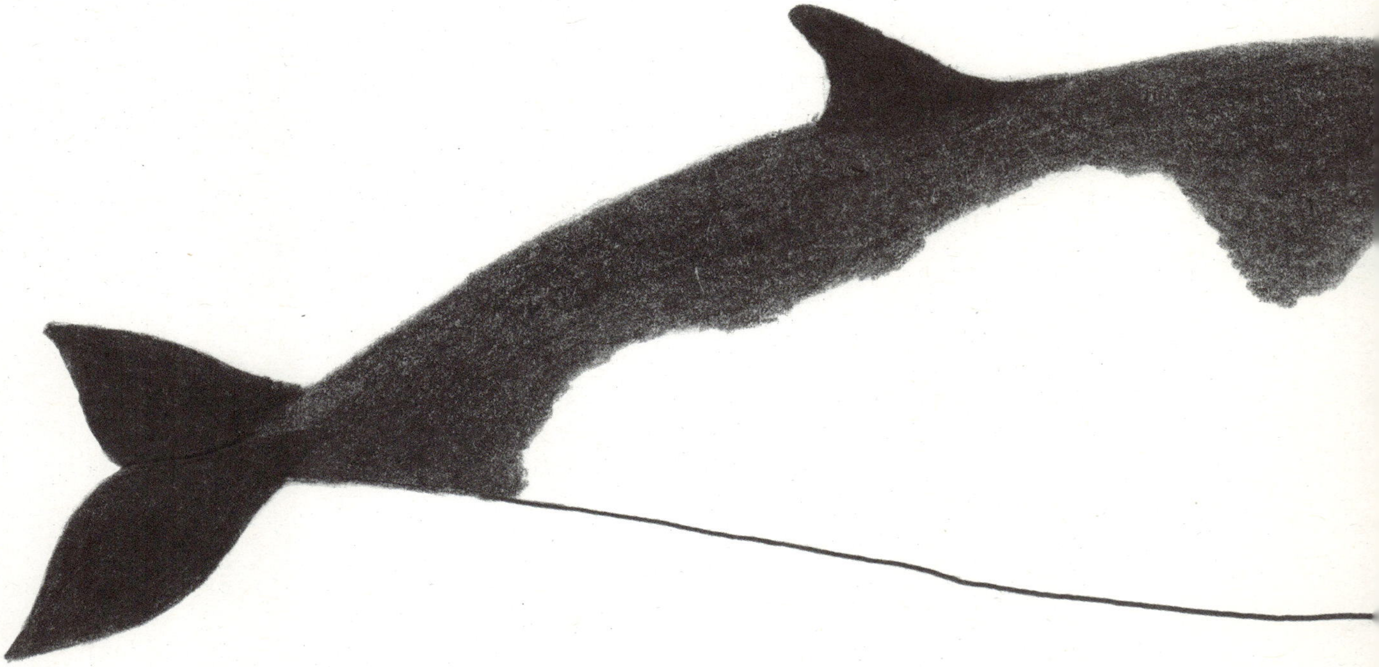

The white colouring of the belly can extend up the sides of the back.

Its **blow** rises up to
3 metres in height,
but we rarely see it.

The colour of the back
varies from black to brown.

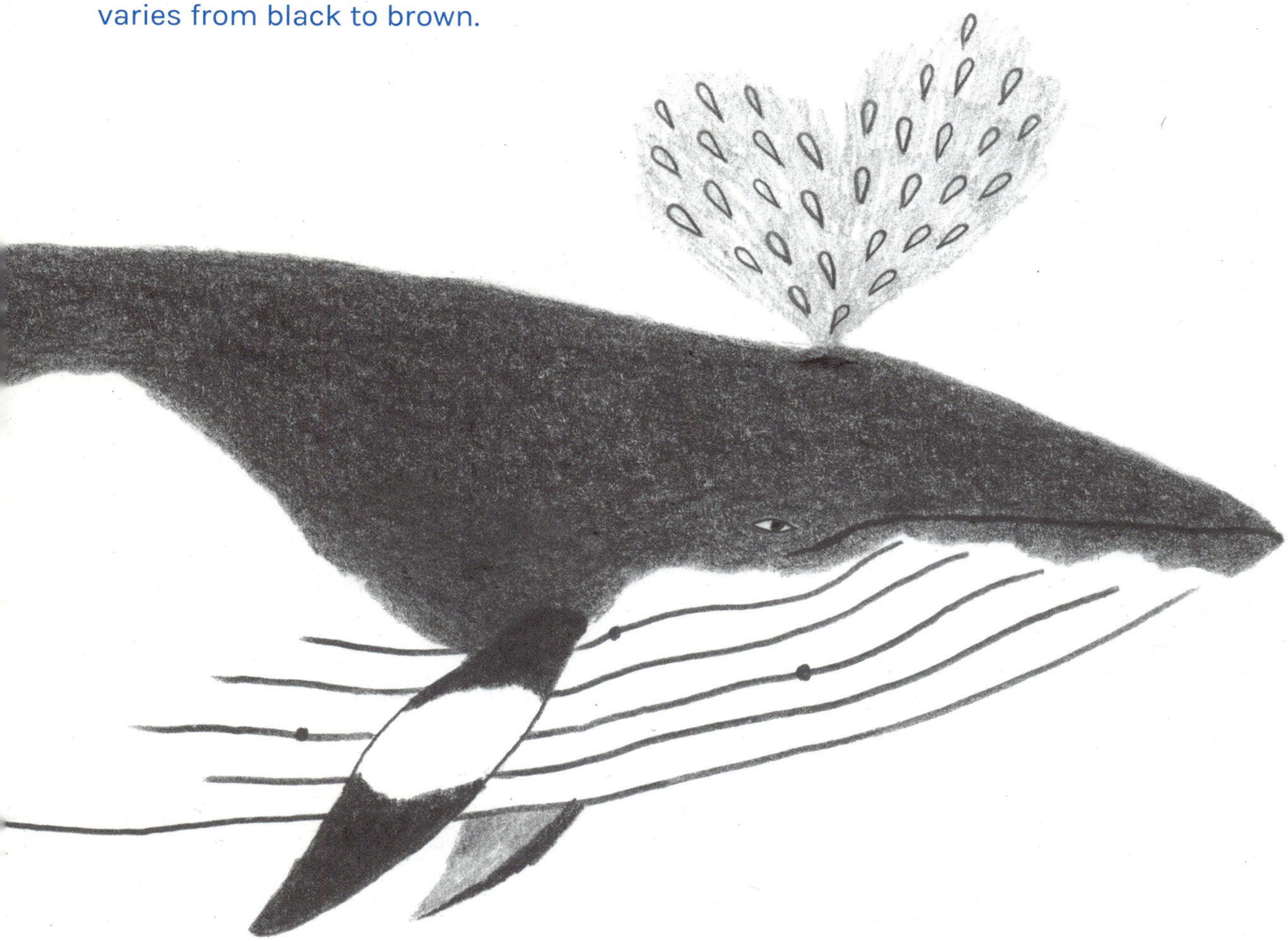

Its most distinctive
hallmark is a white patch
on the **pectoral fins**.

Its name says it all: it is the smallest whale of its family.
They are very curious creatures, often spotting and chasing a boat, wondering what kind of animal it might be. But if they smell the scent of danger, they can escape so quickly that you wouldn't even realize that they had gone!
They often par up with seagulls as fishing buddies, they hold huge feasts together.

Sperm whale

Physeter macrocephalus
Order: Cetacea
Suborder: Odontoceti
Family: Physeteroidea

Length: 11-18 metres
Weight: 20-50 tonnes

It has a rounded hump similar to a **dorsal fin**.

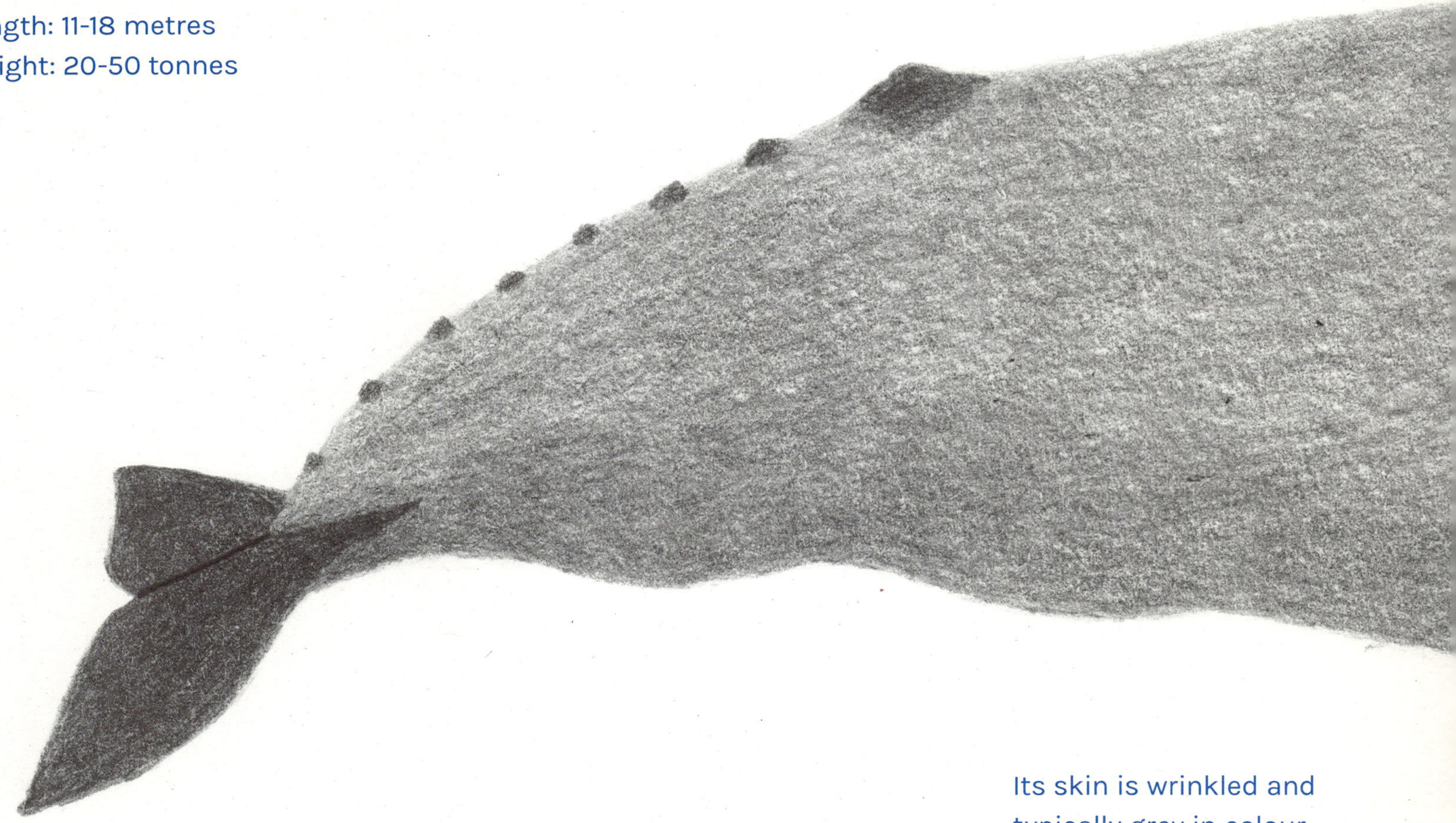

Its skin is wrinkled and typically grey in colour.

The large **tail fin** has a triangular shape.

Its **head** is enormous and usually covered with scars, caused by fighting between males.

It has a characteristic **blow**: it is projected forwards around 5 metres in length and 2 metres in height.

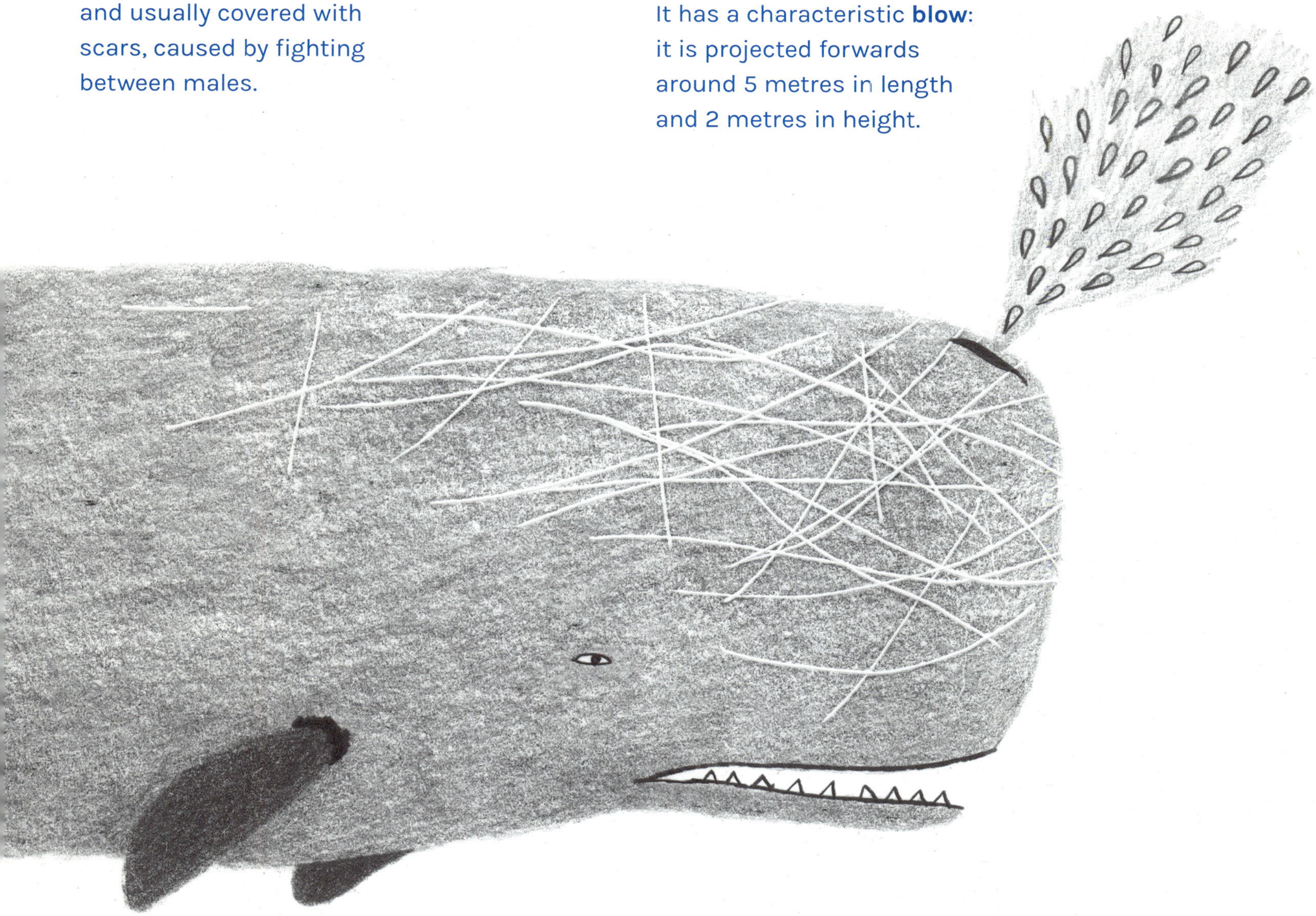

How can you have not heard about Moby Dick, the white sperm whale from the book? This whale is the largest of all toothed whales. In fact, we call it a whale because of its size, even if it is closer in all other respects to a dolphin. Sperm whales are especially good at diving. They can reach 3000 metres below sea in search for squid, holding their breath even for two hours.

Killer whale

Orcinus orca
Order: Cetacea
Suborder: Odontoceti
Family: Delphinidae

Length: 5.5-10 metres
Weight: 2.6-9 tonnes

They have unmistakable colouring: completely black, except for a white belly and spot above the eye.

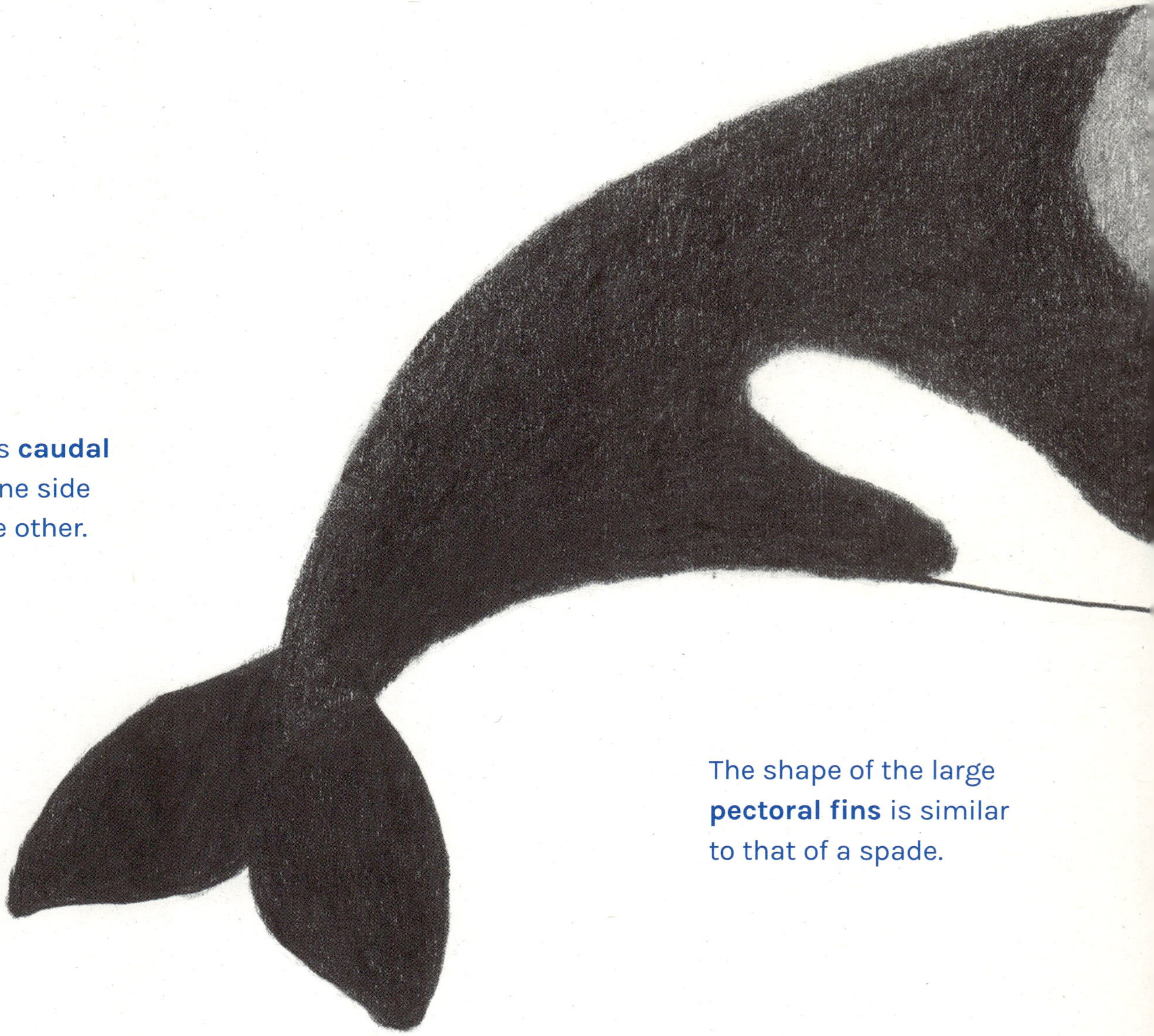

The killer whale's **caudal fin** is black on one side and white on the other.

The shape of the large **pectoral fins** is similar to that of a spade.

The **dorsal fin** is particularly developed in males: it can be up to 2 metres tall.

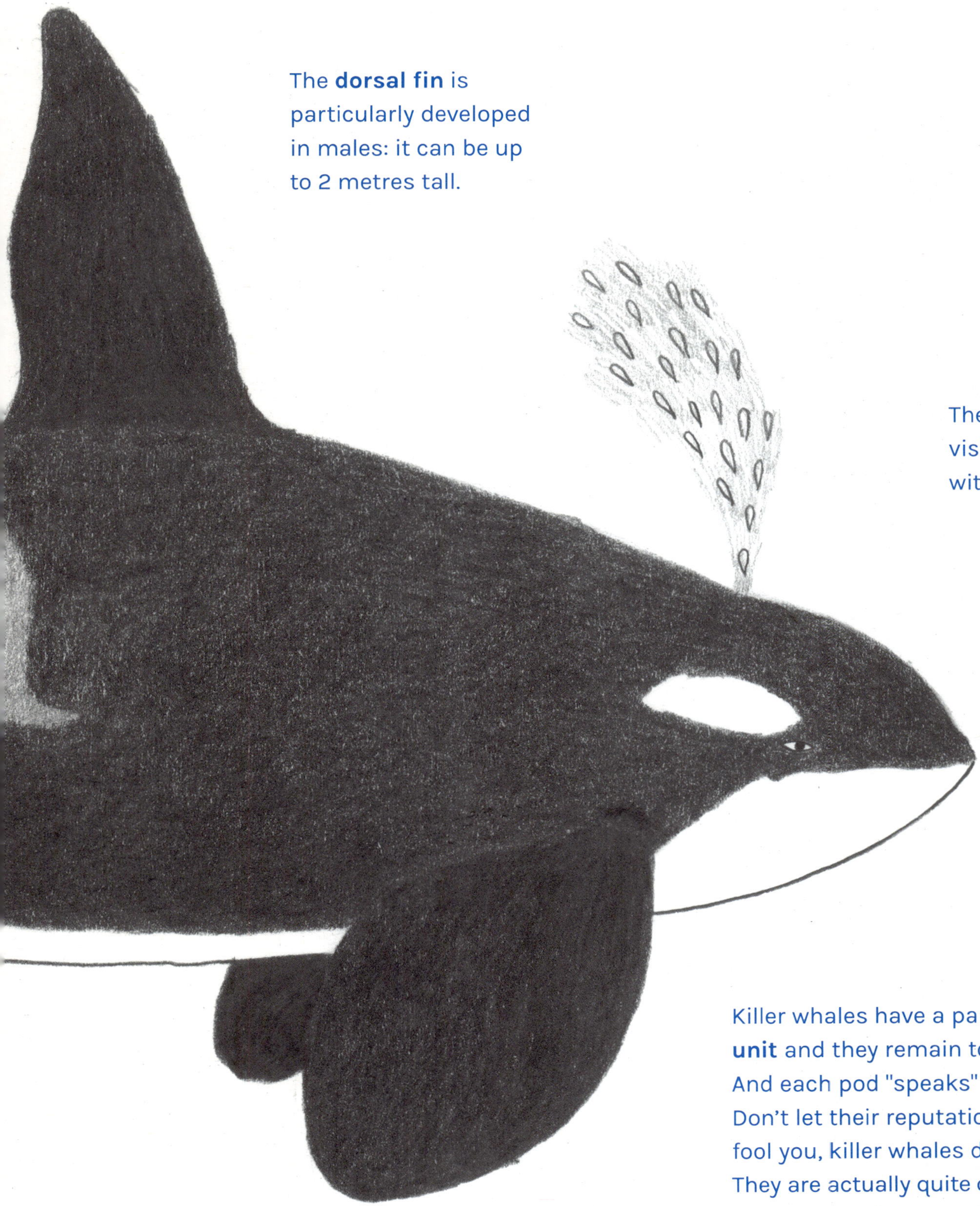

The **blow** is especially visible when in contact with cold air.

Killer whales have a particularly close **family unit** and they remain together for a lifetime. And each pod "speaks" its own special **dialect**! Don't let their reputation as ferocious beasts fool you, killer whales don't attack humans. They are actually quite curious and sometimes even approach us. But if there is a seal or penguin nearby, they certainly won't stand on ceremony.

isiaurbino

Thesis for First Level Academic Diploma

Graphic Design and Visual Communication

Student: Antinori Andrea

Supervisor: Professor Silvana Sola

Winter session, Academic year 2013-2014

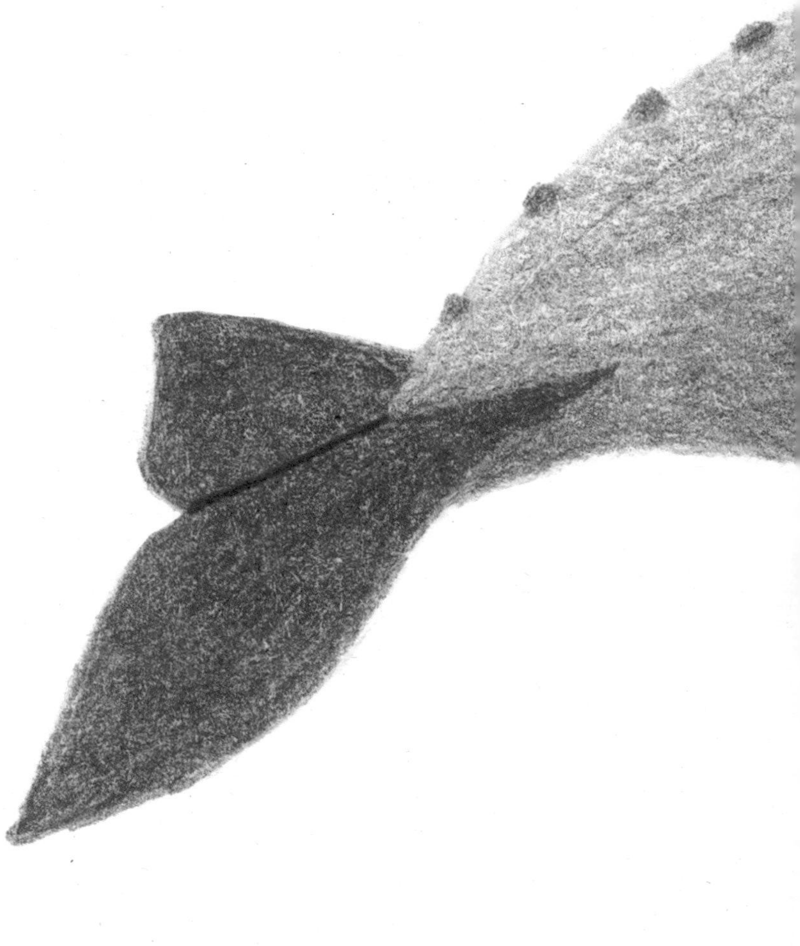

Andrea Antinori

A book about whales

Book design
Andrea Antinori & corrainiStudio

Texts and drawings by
Andrea Antinori

Translation by
David Kelly

We would like to thank Stefano Angelini
Manager of the educational services of the
Acquarium of Genoa

Printed in Italy by
Arti Grafiche Castello, Viadana (Mn)
March 2016

Maurizio Corraini s.r.l.
Via Ippolito Nievo, 7/A
46100 Mantova
Tel. 0039 0376 322753
Fax 0039 0376 365566
e-mail: info@corraini.com
www.corraini.com

Thanks to Luciano Perondi, Silvana Sola, Lorenzo Bravi, Elisa Dalla Battista, Camilla e Gianfranco Marchioni, Maura Benedetti, Varinia Verdecchia for their support and contribution to this project.